Catholicism in America

Catholicism
in America

A SERIES OF ARTICLES FROM

The Commonweal

HARCOURT, BRACE AND COMPANY, NEW YORK

DESIGNED BY ROBERT JOSEPHY

PRINTED IN THE UNITED STATES OF AMERICA

THE ESSAYS assembled in this book first appeared during 1953 as a series of articles in *The Commonweal*, a weekly review published and edited in New York by lay Catholics. Like *The Commonweal*, none of the contributors to this volume is empowered in any way to speak officially for the Church. They are, with two exceptions, Catholic laymen who have undertaken merely to set down their own thoughts on various aspects of American Catholic life. They do not pretend to have produced, even jointly, anything like a full portrait of American Catholicism. Such a portrait would undoubtedly put much greater emphasis on the tremendous spiritual vitality of the Church in the United States. It would focus more attention on the manifold charitable and religious activities carried on by the clergy and religious orders. Undoubtedly, even in dealing with the laity, it would point up other heartening aspects of American Catholicism which even Catholics themselves are inclined to take for granted. But that full portrait has yet to be painted. This collection represents no more than the thinking of a group of Catholic laymen, many of whom have never met each other, on a variety of matters affecting the Church in America and, by that token, affecting America itself.

The Editors of The Commonweal

CONTENTS

Contents

Catholicism in America

George N. Shuster

FOREWORD

THE MAKERS of this book, of whom it may fortunately be said that they live in a time when angels are less timorous than they used to be, are concerned with a situation which is as central from the point of view of speculation about the future of the United States as it often seems remote from everyday routine. A Catholic may go about in nearly every part of this country without encountering so much as a lifted eyebrow, even if perchance he be a priest and wear a Roman collar. But if he wants an argument, one is to be had anywhere, without even the formality of dropping a hat; and he will then learn that the Church to which he belongs is an object of fear, suspicion, resentment, and more or less abrasive jocosity. He may then be led to compare himself with General Grant, who told the nation on the occasion of his second inauguration as President that he had been made "the subject of abuse and slander scarcely ever equaled in political history." To be sure, historians tell us that the General would have made no such comment if he had studied what had been said about some of his precursors with the requisite care; and in like manner a Catholic, if he putters around a little in the chronicle of American invective, will find that he has been a target for only his fair share of it. It may be added that he has used it himself, now and then, with uninhibited vigor.

The Catholic Church is so mighty and flourishing an institution that its faithful must expect to be asked challenging questions. To begin with, it is international, yes, supranational in character, and therefore perennially runs afoul of all those for whom the United States is everything there is of the world. Here it maintains an educational enterprise that has no rival save the public-school system. Publishers of Catholic books, papers, and periodicals reach an audience of millions and there is seemingly no limit to the opportunities available to them. Far more impressive still is the totality of the Catholic clerical establishment, with its powerful hierarchy, its thousands of parish priests, and its ever-increasing community of religious orders, ranging all the way from contemplative Trappists to mercifully active Little Sisters of the Poor. For all this there is required a quantity of real estate and other property holdings that would impress even the members of the Du Pont and Ford families.

One query in particular is put by the contributors in this volume as well as by many others: What do Catholics intend to do about their neighbors, as soon as they have acquired adequate power? For example, were their clergy able to command the support of, say, three out of every five of the citizens of this country, instead of one out of every five, as at present, would they proceed to abolish those provisions of the Constitution which preclude the establishment of a religion and insure the freedom of all? The question cannot be dismissed as purely academic. There are parts of the world where Catholic majorities do curb the rights and privileges of dissidents. In the second place, individual Catholics sometimes talk and act as if they cannot wait for the day when they will be taking over the business of the country and making short shrift of dissenters. I cannot attempt to describe the manner in which the contributors to this book deal with the matter, but will add that the discussion is on an unusually high level of pertinence and wit.

Most of them concern themselves with problems growing out of Catholic life in the United States at the present time. No one should blink at the fact that religion is meaningless unless those who profess it believe that it can answer life's most elemental question: What is man on this earth for, and how can he succeed in doing what is expected of him? Catholic, Protestant, and Jew sincerely feel that their beliefs are sacred and dependable. They want others to share this certainty with them. How, then, shall one avoid surrendering any jot or tittle of one's conviction while respecting the commitment of another? This has always been a crucial problem, and we can only hope that it will continue to be one. We cannot deal with it on the basis of some such premise as that we all see through a glass darkly, and therefore one guess is as good as another. We must say, rather, with great humility and sincerity: This is the truth as I see it and therefore I shall abide by it; but since God is the Lord of Love, Who has indicated that no man may judge any other, I shall follow His command in this respect also. This resolution may often be as difficult to abide by as is the precept that an enemy is to be loved. But a Christian, at least, cannot gainsay that both are written indelibly on his marching orders.

Reinhold Niebuhr addresses himself to one important cleavage between Catholics and Protestants. The latter generally do not endorse the Catholic emphasis on Natural Law, discovery of (or, if you will, attachment to) which was a major

achievement of antique philosophy. And, indeed, throughout
the whole of the contemporary world, insofar as it is still
religious-minded, the debate is between the protagonists of
faith rooted in reason and the apostles of a faith that distrusts
reason as a guide to ultimate truth. That is why, in the con-
test with secularism, which respects only its own definition of
reason, Catholic, Protestant, and Jewish positions are necessarily different. And since the Catholic is one who cherishes
the tradition of reason, of the perennial philosophy, his success will of necessity depend somewhat, at least, upon how
he brings the force of the intellect to bear upon philosophical,
sociological, and, more narrowly, scientific phenomena and
the inferences therefrom.

To what extent do Catholics succeed in doing so in this
country? How deeply interested are they in scientific research
or humanistic endeavor or the practice of the fine arts? Does
the heritage they carry with them from immigrant days include items which they ought long since to have left on the
town dump? It is, for example, a fact that the Catholic population has not made the contribution to the study of the
natural sciences that its numbers suggest, whereas it has
given a proportionately larger share of distinguished practi-
tioners to medicine; and the reasons why this is so should be
unearthed and evaluated with complete objectivity. Having
some years ago dealt with a comparable problem and as a
result ignited any number of firecrackers, I think I may say
that the context in which the question is put today is notably
different from what it was during the '20s. The contribution
being made at present to the study of the sciences by Catholic universities is plainly discernible, even if it is far less
than might be desired. It is now, to cite Mr. Pleasants, one-
tenth of what might be expected from a comparable group

of non-Catholics. I fancy that much the same situation obtains in social science and humanistic scholarship.

But the issue that transcends all others is that of the relationship between the clergy and the laity. It is on the whole a good relationship, though nowhere else are the debts incurred as a result of old wars incidental to immigration still costing so much in terms of interest and amortization. To be sure, the recurrent repayments are by no means as important as writers like the late Thomas Sugrue were wont to assume. On the whole, Catholic clergymen have remained close to their people and have served them loyally; they have not all got on the bandwagons of the prosperous bourgeoisie; they have stayed where they are needed, whether it be in stockyards neighborhoods or in drab suburban settlements. For this they merit respect and affection, though occasionally the expression of both may have undesirable overtones of sentimentality. Nevertheless there obviously exists a most deplorable gap between the educated, civic-minded layman and his priests. This is seldom occasioned by excessive broadmindedness or sin on the part of the laity—indeed, it often seems to me that the interested layman is more dead set against sin than are the clergy. The dissonance springs rather from living in different dimensions of intellectual experience. For the active lay citizen, life is fashioned by discussions in which the clergy (exception having been duly made for diverse members of some religious orders) do not share. The habit of give-and-take which is formed in the one is scarcely compensated for by the other's dedication to withdrawal. Why, then, should it be surprising that there are occasions when priests, emerging from isolation and speaking their pieces, may well seem (regardless of the varying colors of their raiment) to the listening laity aught else than inspired prophets?

There is no need for illustrative material at this point. The deplorable result is that a sizable minority of American Catholics grows restless and dissatisfied, and that, alas, it happens again and again that the ties to the faith itself therefore grow weak. For those outside, something akin to scandal often ensues. That all this is wholly unnecessary and accordingly tragic is demonstrated clearly by the great, salutary change that has taken place in essential Catholic journalism edited and in large part written by an emerging realistic and far-sighted younger clergy. A tide is discernible, and we may well hope that it will be a regenerating one. For if American Catholics can at long last rid themselves of tabus and temptations to seek recourse in pressure politics, they can help to make the social and intellectual traditions of their Church meaningful to Americans generally. If this book is, as I think, a notable reflection of this upward movement, it may well be that when historians look back upon the date of its publication they will award it a commendation for sincerity and earnestness, for faith and hope and charity, which those who have written it do not now fancy that they deserve.

William P. Clancy

CATHOLICISM
IN AMERICA

To BEGIN a discussion of Catholicism in America with the announced aim of being "critical" and "objective" suggests the danger of various misunderstandings. Non-Catholics may see in it an attempt to "Americanize" the Church by watering down its dogmas to make them more palatable to "liberal" tastes. Catholics may fear that the ghosts of modernism, exorcised by Pope Pius X, may loom again in such a topic. It might be well, then, to lessen the danger by indicating at the outset the limits of the discussion. They are implied in a famous observation by the late Cardinal Gibbons: "The American Church must of its very nature be the same as in Rome or Jerusalem; but in the same manner in which its garb takes on the color of its surroundings, it must also be American."

For a Catholic to discuss "Catholicism in America" is therefore not to discuss Catholicism *as such*. The very nature of the Church, as it understands itself and is understood by its members, makes such a discussion impossible. The Church, in its dogma and sacraments, essentially transcends both time and place. It knows as little of time and place as it knows of Jew or Gentile, freeman or slave. It knows only Christ and His Revelation—the same yesterday, today, and forever.

9

But the Church is not only essentially transcendent; it is also, through its members, incarnate in a given time and place. Through its members, it affects a culture and is affected, for better or worse, by the local conditions and challenges that its members meet. In this sense it assumes that "garb" of which Gibbons spoke. In this sense we can distinguish "Catholicism" in France, in Ireland, in Italy—or in America. Distinguishing, we can see that differences in attitude and behavior, sometimes minor, sometimes important, exist in the Catholic climate in various times and places. To examine the climate of Catholic opinion and attitudes in American culture, its strengths and weaknesses, is the purpose of this collection.

Such an examination does not seem a gratuitous undertaking. Recent controversies have made it increasingly necessary. It may be true that it is only the extremists among both Catholics and non-Catholics whose public statements, books, and magazines have excited current suspicions, but, extremists aside, there are still real problems to be faced. Many non-Catholics, men of good will, are sincerely disturbed by what they see as a threat to democratic values from a Catholic minority, and many Catholics, also men of good will, are troubled by the threat to spiritual values that the challenge of liberal secularism offers.

To pretend that the fears on either side are completely without foundation in fact, and that no ambiguities exist in the present situation, seems singularly unreal. And to leave the discussion to Mr. Paul Blanshard on the one side and to his Catholic counterparts on the other seems singularly unwise.

The problem of Catholicism in America, as seen in its extreme form, might be stated as follows: Catholics see the

Church as the only force left strong enough to combat an increasingly arrogant secularist invasion of culture. On every side they see challenged those spiritual values without which civilization becomes mere organized barbarism: in education, in the arts, in entertainment, in politics, in every major sphere of public and private life, neopaganism, frequently masquerading under the names of "liberalism" and "freedom," threatens the foundations of morality, truth, decency, and public order. To preserve not only the values proper to their own religion but even those basic to the Natural Law itself, Catholics believe that they must oppose the extension of secularism going under the name of "democracy."

Many non-Catholics, on the other hand, complain that Catholics in this country, for all their pious protestations of loyalty to the "American way of life," constantly exhibit their contempt for ordinary democratic procedures. They say that Catholics, through their organizations, political influence, and pressure groups, everywhere seek to impose their own minority will upon the majority—and that they frequently succeed. Convinced that Catholics are authoritarian and antiliberal by nature, they fear that eventual Catholic dominance in American culture would mark the end of a free society in the United States.

Unfortunately, these conflicting fears even in this extreme form can easily find evidence to support them. By reading various manifestoes of American "liberalism" (some issued from high, ivy-covered places), the Catholic can find strong confirmation of his fears of doctrinaire democracy. And a weekly examination of certain sections of the Catholic press would provide Mr. Blanshard with footnotes for many future volumes. For there is a type of monolithic "democracy" being preached in the United States to which no Catholic could ever subscribe. And some Catholics draw politically and culturally authoritarian implications from their faith that free men necessarily find abhorrent. Interestingly enough, the roots of both these attitudes can be found, I believe, in a common ground. Strikingly dissimilar at first glance, they seem to be, on examination, essentially alike. In their extreme form they are both the fruit of that totalitarian spirit which, hating diversity, demands that all existence be made over to conform to its own vision.

Whether the vision be of time or of eternity is of little matter. The spirit that gives it birth is the same. It is, under various guises, an attempt to overextend one level of reality into the proper domain of another—to subjugate things. As such, it represents a sort of original sin against the hierarchy of creation itself—against things-as-they-are.

The two opposing views—of the Church as a "weapon" to be used against the advance of secularist culture, and of the Church as a threat to democratic values—are frequently and heatedly expressed in controversies over the use of "pressure tactics" by Catholics in public affairs. And in the positions sometimes taken by both sides in these controversies that totalitarian spirit which is the antagonists' hidden bond becomes evident. An examination of the difficulties and ambiguities involved in the "pressure group" argument reveals, therefore, some of the basic problems of Catholicism in America.

The initial difficulty is that "pressure" is a loaded word, applied ordinarily to groups whose activities one wishes, by its use, to condemn. Americans for Democratic Action lobbying for public health insurance is probably not, in its own view, acting as a "pressure group"; the American Medical Association lobbying against public health insurance, in its own view, is probably not acting as a "pressure group" either. Each is likely to think of itself as acting patriotically; the one to achieve "social justice," the other to preserve "free enterprise." But each is likely to think the other a "pressure group." Application of the term depends, usually, on one's prejudices and predilections.

Catholics are no exception to this. Although discussion of Catholic "pressure" is widespread, few Catholics care to admit that it exists. They would rather insist that those organized Catholic activities which some call "pressure" are nothing of the kind but rather clear and simple cases of promoting morality, securing justice, or suppressing scandal—all praiseworthy efforts which only an enemy of religion would denigrate.

I think it important, therefore, that the definition of "pressure group" be precise, and it seems to me a definition that has nothing to do, essentially, with who composes such groups, what their motivation may be, what methods they employ, or what merits their goal may have. These are important but secondary questions; they arise when one asks whether a particular pressure group is good or bad. Essentially, a pressure group is simply one that attempts to influence the course of affairs external to itself through the methods of organized persuasion and propaganda.

To admit that a pressure group exists does not, therefore, imply that one necessarily disapproves of it. On the contrary, though we may dislike the organized influence of those with whom we disagree and find it polemically convenient to characterize it as "pressure," we must admit, I think, that such influence—pressure or not—is a necessary part of the democratic process.

In a free society not only individuals but groups as well

have a right to make themselves heard and a duty to work toward those ends that they believe necessary for society's good. To imagine that this right and this duty can effectively be exercised without the use of pressure is to postulate a hopelessly romantic, hopelessly utopian State, one in which the citizens are more eminently virtuous, educable, and wise than in any democracy that ever was or ever can be.

Much of the heated talk about pressure groups is, therefore, largely meaningless insofar as it assumes that to name them is to condemn them. In every free society there are times when men with the courage of their convictions must resort to pressure tactics—to public protest, propaganda, and demonstration—in order to achieve their ends. This is part of "democracy"; it goes with the functioning of the real world.

The Church has always resisted quietism; it has never despised the world. It is in the world, and is concerned with the world's good—even its natural good. Those who cry "pressure" each time Catholics seek to influence society betray a poor understanding not only of the Church but of democracy as well. For in a democracy the interplay of conflicting forces must not only be tolerated, it must be welcomed.

The question of pressure groups in American life should not be posed as a categorical one; it is not a question of whether they should be, but rather of what forms they can legitimately take. It is a question, ultimately, of prudence.

It is not easy for two societies whose ends are divergent to live together. The long history of the Church's struggles with princes and of the princes' struggles with the Church underlines this. Concordats between the papacy and civil power have been a classic means of achieving some *modus vivendi* between the two societies, each jealous of its own rights. But concordats are not popular today, particularly in countries where there is great concern over "separation of Church and State." The ancient problem of the two societies remains, and its resolution is still far from complete.

The use of political pressure by Catholic groups is a major—perhaps *the* major—aspect of this problem in the United States today. It has divided Catholic from non-Catholic and, in specific instances, Catholic from Catholic. There are, I think, two reasons for this—one obvious, the other more subtle.

The obvious reason is the rise in the United States of what Father John Courtney Murray has called the "new Nativism," the modern counterreligion of democratic absolutism. Mr. Paul Blanshard is its most celebrated prophet but he most certainly is not its founder, for it is the contemporary manifestation, in American terms, of an old idea. Its roots are in the Enlightenment; it had its classic expression in the French Revolution, and its hangover in the Third French Republic. It is the idea of the completely autonomous, thoroughly laicized, antireligious State.

In this State, religion may be tolerated with a certain degree of enlightened benevolence, but its influence must be confined to the sacristy. Any attempt by it to go forth from the sacristy, to make its voice heard in public affairs, any real challenge, in short, that it may offer to the State, must be resisted. Because this State is profoundly antipluralist and hence profoundly totalitarian, it hates diversity and, especially, it hates transcendence. The area of challenge it will tolerate in its public life is limited to what falls within the sphere of its own philosophy; it cannot, therefore, tolerate the transcendent challenge of religion. The cry of "pressure" which is automatically raised in America each time a Catholic group attempts to influence public affairs is a sign of this. It is an indication of how far the "new Nativism" has penetrated our national life.

This is, I say, an obvious reason for the controversial aspect of Catholic "pressure." It has little to do, however, with the real problems involved. It is external to them and concerns the peculiar totalitarian mentality of those who (in the name of "democracy") protest any assertion of religious values in the affairs of the State.

The more subtle reason why the use of pressure is at the heart of the question of Catholicism in America—and is perhaps its most controversial aspect—is part of the ancient problem of the two societies, each with its own ends, the Church and the State. As we have noted, a classic formula for achieving some *modus vivendi* between them was a concordat in which the rights of each were defined, guaranteed, and limited by mutual consent. But this device would not solve the problem as it exists in the United States, for we have here a unique historic situation. It is not the old Confessional State, but it is not the laicized State of the Revolution either. It is a State in which the civil and ecclesiastical jurisdiction are clearly distinguished but yet are not set in opposition to each other. As Father Murray has written (in *Theological Studies,* June 1949):

There is [in the United States] a unique historical realization of the "lay" state—unique because this lay state is not laicized or laicizing on the Continental model. This lay state does not pretend to be The Whole—an absolutely autonomous, all-embracing religio-political magnitude with its own quasi-religious content. . . . On the contrary, there is in the First Amendment a recognition of the primacy of the spiritual—a recognition that is again unique, in that it is a recognition of the primacy of the spiritual life of the human person, as a value supreme over any values incorporated in the State. . . . In other words, the First Amendment rescues the American State from the monism which has characterized the modern laicized State. Its premise is the Christian dualist concept of man; and it recognizes that a dyarchy therefore governs the life of man and of society. . . .

In such a lay State, Father Murray observes, "there is first the free obedience of the Christian conscience to the magisterial and jurisdictional authority of the Church; there is secondly the free participation of the citizen, as a Christian, in the institutions whereby all the processes of temporal life are directed to their proper ends," therefore, "in the native structure of the American system the citizen-of-religious-conscience is placed in the mediating position between Church and State. The Church is free to form the consciences of her members and they as citizens are free to conform the life of the City to the demands of their consciences. . . ."

There is a great burden here. For Christians, as citizens, to be "in the mediating position between Church and State" is a terrible responsibility. For them to be "free to conform the life of the City to the demands of their consciences" is a historic challenge. Father Murray recalls that the concept of Catholic Action, as elaborated by the recent popes, has been called the "modern form of relations between Church and State." The Christian citizen of the modern lay State can thus be said to have inherited, personally, the function of the concordat. In addition to being Christian-citizen he must be diplomat too, reconciling wherever possible the two cities of which he is a member, maintaining the principles of each without compromising his loyalty to either. This is, obviously, a most delicate task.

The use of pressure has been one of the means by which

Catholics living in the United States have undertaken this task of conforming the life of the city to the demands of their consciences. They have thus been quick to argue, to demonstrate, to protest, to picket, to boycott when they have believed basic moral issues were at stake. In this they have insisted they were asserting their democratic rights, and have resented the charge that in doing so they were somehow undermining democracy.

The resentment, in many cases, has been justified. But does it touch the real problem? Granted that the use of pressure is, in itself, part of the democratic process; granted that Catholics picketing, protesting, boycotting are within their constitutional rights; granted that the outcry against them is often the result of antireligious bias rather than of a real concern for freedom; granted all this, the real problem of whether the use of pressure is *appropriate* to the Christian-citizen's role in the lay State remains unanswered.

I think we must say that in many specific instances the use of Catholic pressure has been neither appropriate, nor expedient, nor prudent. And for this reason: It has frequently been exercised without reference to the historical, cultural, and political framework within which it must operate—the framework of a pluralist-liberal American society. Anxious to assert the validity of absolute moral values in the temporal order, Catholic groups have sometimes forgotten that the temporal order, as it is here and now, has its own exigencies, its own validities. They must not demand of it an absolute quality that it cannot return.

Organized Catholic efforts in the labor movement, in the fight for racial equality, in the struggle for social justice have undoubtedly involved many cases of pressure, but little has been said of them. No one, for example, has protested that in fighting against restrictive covenants or demanding the right of labor to organize, Catholic groups were in a conspiracy to subvert American freedom. There is, I think, a reason for this. In these areas the Catholic effort has been made for the same basic reasons as in other more controversial areas. It has been the attempt to apply Christian principle in the temporal order, and as part of the attempt certain demands on the temporal order were made—but with a difference. The demands in these cases could not be interpreted as born of self-interest. And they did not ask of the temporal order what it could not give. They were consonant with its own nature and its own ends.

In other areas of American life, however, the Catholic temptation (which we might call the "moral temptation") has been to demand of the temporal order that absolute quality which is proper to the Church. When this temptation has expressed itself through pressure, particularly in the realm of ideas and the arts, the result has been often unfortunate and sometimes disastrous. Pressure, as a justifiable form of Catholic activity, must be exercised in reference to the ends of the temporal society in which it operates as well as by inspiration of the eternal values from which it springs. In its use Catholics must not set the two societies in opposition. They must not ask that the State become the Church.

But they sometimes seem to do this. If they pressure the State to ban a book or a movie as "objectionable" and base their demand on criteria which the State, qua State, cannot know ("sacrilege" is the now classic example of this), they justify, however innocently, the fears of those who see Catholic influence as a threat to America's free traditions. It is not enough that something be *true* to justify Catholics demanding its enforcement in the temporal order. It must also be *possible* in terms of that order's own traditions and ends. This is the great lesson that apparently has yet to be thoroughly learned.

A key to its mastery and, in a larger sense, a key to the whole problem of Catholicism in a democratic society, is provided by a distinction of the planes on which Christians can act in the world. This is a distinction which Jacques Maritain has made with great brilliance in his *True Humanism* and I think that to recall it—along with its implications for our culture—is of special value here.

The planes of action as Maritain distinguishes them are: first, the spiritual, which is the plane of eternal life and of the Church; second, the temporal, which is the plane of the earthly city and of those activities that are directed to this city's good; and, third, the "mixed," which is the plane on which the spiritual and the temporal join.

On the first plane, the spiritual, Maritain reminds us, our action must be that of Christians *as such,* for this is the plane of the Church, of her dogma and sacraments. Here, therefore, Catholics must act together.

The same may be said for the activity of Catholics on the third, the "mixed" plane, where the spiritual becomes directly involved with the temporal. Here the higher good, the spiritual, must always be the determining object of the Christian's action. In such situations (one thinks of marriage, education, etc.) where a real conflict might occur between the claims of the spiritual and of the temporal goods, the Christian's obligation is obvious.

On the second plane, however, that of the temporal, the city of man, our action cannot be that of Christians *as such* but only that of Christian citizens of the earthly city. For here the determining object of action is not, properly, eternal

life but rather the temporal good of the city. And, for that
reason, the rule for action here must ordinarily be not unity
but diversity.

For Christians to seek a false unity in the order of temporal action would be, as Maritain points out, contrary to the
very nature of things, a dangerous "political materialization
of religious energies." And, although Catholics should take
positions on temporal matters "in the light and illumination
of their Catholic conscience," it would be intolerable if in so
doing they should "claim to speak in the name of Catholicism
and implied that all Catholics as such should follow their
road."

As Maritain concludes, there is indeed a judgment of Catholicism on political and cultural questions, but "this judgment only bears on certain principles seen from a very lofty
angle, on which these questions depend, or on certain spiritual values which they imply." It will not tell the individual
Catholic what attitude he should take up on most of the specific temporal questions—political, cultural, educational—with
which he will be concerned during his lifetime. There is not,
nor can there be, a "Catholic" attitude on these. There is only
the attitude of the particular Catholic.

The American environment is the heir, par excellence, of
those dreams of material progress, human perfectibility, and
an earthly utopia that bemused the genius of Europe during
most of the eighteenth and nineteenth centuries. It is a culture which, perhaps more than any other in history, has
sought to canonize the temporal. Having escaped the tragedies that awakened Europe from the Enlightenment's dream,
America continues to enjoy that dream. In this sense, the most
"progressive" of countries is an anachronism in the modern
world.

The major modern spokesmen for a materialistic utopia have been the liberal prophets. Through the Enlightenment's "reason" and its weapon, scientism, they have hoped to make the world over in their own image. Their vision has been that of the earthly paradise, and they have sought to include within that vision the totality of human experience.

It is a vision which religious men continue to find not only inadequate and naïve but basically terrifying. They are convinced (and modern history fortifies their conviction) that it is a vision which, rejecting absolute morality, must ultimately result in rejecting man himself. They fear that any abandonment of absolute spiritual values for the sake of a material "progress" is more likely to end in Hitler's jungle than in Rousseau's garden.

It has been remarked that the tyranny of a democratic majority is the most terrible of all tyrannies—"The absolute ruler may be a Nero, but he is sometimes Titus or Marcus Aurelius; the people is often Nero, and never Marcus Aurelius"—and this may be true. Yet, even a majority tyranny, if the majority subscribe to some absolute standard of morality, will be somehow limited and humanized. The tyranny of a majority that rejects all absolute morality, however, is a refinement in horror which it has taken the modern world to discover. It is this horror which the democratic absolutists seem to offer in the name of enlightenment, and it is against this threat that religious men react.

The difficulty is that their reaction to the threat and the slogans of doctrinaire secularism sometimes becomes an equally doctrinaire spiritualism. Their challenge to those who distrust the rights of the eternal is to counterchallenge the rights of the temporal. In such a climate, genuine values, both temporal and eternal, are the victims.

I think that the growth of such a climate is the basic problem of "Catholicism in America" today. As the American environment grows increasingly secularized, Catholics grow more fearful for the survival of spiritual values. And as they do, they attempt to impose a unity and authority on areas of life in which they can make no legitimate spiritual demands. It is a vicious circle. The secularists provide the religious "integralists" with ammunition to be used against the claims of the temporal, and the "integralists," in their turn, give the secularists ammunition for use against the rights of the spiritual. Mr. Blanshard and certain spokesmen for an "integral," "militant" Catholicism really owe each other much.

It would not seem especially appropriate for a Catholic to advise his non-Catholic fellow citizens on what they should do about the threat he sees from their quarter. For one thing, there is probably little he can do about their problem directly. He can merely point it out and warn against it. The hope is that they themselves will see that the monolith of democratic absolutism is at least as terrifying a threat to free men as any that may come from Catholics—more terrifying, indeed, because it is more immediate.

But it might be appropriate for a Catholic to recommend to his fellow Catholics meditation on a passage from Lord Acton: "In politics as in science the Church need not seek her own ends. She will obtain them if she encourages the pursuit of the ends of science, which are truth, and of the State, which are liberty." One of the great needs in the American Catholic climate is, I believe, an increased respect for the truth in Acton's observation, which is, ultimately, the truth of Maritain's distinctions on the action proper to Christians on the temporal plane.

Catholics in America do not lack a zeal for the spiritual.

They are orthodox; they seem, on the whole, united and loyal in those things which pertain to eternal life. And on the "mixed" plane of action they seem mature too. Against the threat of secularism they have maintained, sometimes heroically, the sanctity of Christian marriage and the integrity of Christian education. But, on the temporal level, they seem sometimes dangerously unaware. In politics, literature, science, and art, they seem strangely unwilling to render the temporal its due, to grant that measure of diversity and freedom proper to it.

There is, perhaps, deep in the Catholic memory, nostalgia for an older, a safer, a more certain temporal order. We may not, all of us, have grown used to the hazards of living within a pluralist culture, and some of our demands, some of our "pressure," may reflect this nostalgia, this immaturity as citizens. As the nostalgia disappears, as we mature, it is to be hoped that our voice may be lowered, our demands grow less strident, and our own sense of vocation—in this time, in this place—may become more secure.

We may realize better that absolutisms cannot be transferred simply from the spiritual to the temporal sphere; that there are large areas of human behavior (those in which most of us operate, practically, all our lives) where an enlightened pragmatism and a respect for tentative judgments are the essential methods of free men; that a "Catholic" position is not always possible. If Catholics in America can learn a more profound respect for the rights of the temporal, and non-Catholic liberals a more basic reverence for the rights of the spiritual, there need be no further threat to democracy or religion from either side. The obligation involved seems to be mutual.

Reinhold Niebuhr

A PROTESTANT LOOKS
AT CATHOLICS

Though the Catholic may find the practice dubious, every discussion of the Catholic Church, at least in America, is bound to begin with the issue of the relation of the Church to a "free society." Such a discussion almost always contains more or less prejudiced views of the resources and defects of the Catholic Church for the achievement and preservation of "democracy." The Catholic may find this American habit dubious because it probably involves an idolatrous estimate of democracy, which lifts a democratic society into the position of an ultimate criterion of value and truth.

Although I share these misgivings, I shall start this non-Catholic estimate of American Catholicism in the same way, first because I regard the preservation of a free society as important, and secondly because all the judgments about the Church by outsiders have, as a matter of fact, this implied or explicit yardstick.

A sympathetic critic of the Church would be bound to begin with this theme, if for no other reason than because he is bound to dispel misconceptions general among his fellow Americans about the relation of the Church to democracy.

25

Catholicism in America

The Church is thought to be antidemocratic, partly because it is authoritarian, and partly because its religious unity appears, at least from the perspective of the multicolored Protestant and secular life, to be politically monolithic.

Partly the misconception rests on stereotypes that identify Catholicism with the political structure of Spain, let us say, rather than with France or the German Rhineland. I must admit that these misconceptions have the one grain of truth that they prove that forces other than those in the Church operated to transmute medieval social structures into modern ones. But they are misconceptions nevertheless because they underestimate the resources of Catholicism for preserving justice and stability in a free society, once established. They are misconceptions because they do not do justice to the role of Catholicism in the free societies in America, France, Germany, and Western Europe. They do not realize, for instance, what a contribution the Catholic conception of the superiority of political authority over the economic process made in avoiding the aberrations of both doctrinaire "free enterprise" economics and contrasting Marxist aberrations. Nor do these criticisms take account of the practical effects of the Church's ability to qualify the class antagonisms in an industrial society by holding the loyalty of the industrial classes and allowing their viewpoints to color the political positions of Catholic political parties. It was this achievement, together with a Christian check on extreme nationalism, that gave Catholicism such a stabilizing influence in an otherwise unstable Weimar Republic, and that determines the creative force of the Catholic parties in modern France and Western Germany.

I say this, though I am grateful that Anglo-Saxon democracy has avoided religious parties, and grateful that Catholic viewpoints have expressed themselves in American life in the voices of such man as the late Philip Murray and the present Secretary of Labor, without the organization of a Catholic party. I believe, in short, that American non-Catholics do not appreciate the tremendous difference between the Church in an unreconstructed medieval social setting and the Church finding a creative place in the moral and political reconstruction of a modern industrial society.

An appreciation of this creative role does not eliminate some of the difficulties which even a friendly critic must experience with the role of the Church in modern society. The Catholic belief that error does not have the same rights as the truth, and its consequent impatience with those democratic practices that seem to arbitrate matters of truth and value by counting noses, is a point of friction between the Church and a democratic society. It can be partly resolved if a distinction is made between matters of truth and morals and matters of detailed application and the technical details involved in the application of moral principles.

I frankly cannot find, in some modern Catholic theory, an adequate consideration of Aquinas' warning that matters of application become increasingly hazardous the further they are removed from principle and involved in adjustment to historical contingency. In this, modern Catholic theory seems to me comparable to modern social science, which does not heed Aristotle's warning that a field of inquiry embodying the historically contingent is not a proper realm for nous but rather for phronesis or "practical wisdom."

Beyond these possible misunderstandings between Catholicism and the ethos of a democracy, there remains the profound difference that democracy, while not determining the truth by the count of noses, is, of course, relativist in the sense that it would take a chance with error rather than give anyone the absolute authority to define the truth. I think this tension could be overcome if it were understood that no democratic political authority can challenge the authority of the Church to define the ultimate truth in its sphere, while it was also understood that the State, that is, the democratic State, was at least provisionally relativist in not permitting any definition of the truth to infringe upon the "rule of majority."

Some of us are frankly a little puzzled to know why it was thought necessary, in such books as Ryan and Boland's *Catholic Principles of Politics,* to disavow the earlier position expounded by the late Cardinal Gibbons and the late Archbishop Ireland, which came to terms with our practical democratic presuppositions, and to insist instead that it was the duty of the State to teach not only religion but the "true religion." This position seems to threaten our nation with the prospects of an established religion, though the fears of non-Catholics are probably unrealistic in view of the qualifications in the Catholic theory.

Some of us hope that the theory will gain ground in the Catholic Church that the State is responsible for the general welfare but not for the salvation of souls. We don't know how respectable or orthodox it is, though it has good parentage. It would eliminate a point of friction between the Church and the traditions of our nation without sacrificing any important claims of the Church.

Next to the problem of the relation of the Church to the State, the problem of the relation of Catholicism to the Protestant Churches is of great moment to us. I am not anxious to apportion degrees of guilt for a deplorable situation for which the blame must probably be divided fairly evenly, but

the relations between Catholics and Protestants in this country are a scandal and an offense against Christian charity.

Last year I was visited by a German Lutheran pastor from
the Rhineland, here on a study tour to acquaint himself with
our life. The presupposition of the visit was that the victors
could instruct the vanquished in every aspect of "democratic"
life, including the relations of the various religious groups.
The German visitor was amazed to find that Catholic-Protestant relations were on the level of professional "love feasts"
in which members of the various traditions exhorted a common audience on the values of co-operation and of mutual
tolerance. But there was nowhere an honest and searching
interchange of thought either on questions that have traditionally separated Catholics and Protestants or on current
issues that are sore points between them in practical politics.

The German pastor contrasted this condition with the community that existed between Protestants and Catholics in the
Rhineland, where he had only recently attended a joint re-
treat under the leadership of the Bishop of Mainz. He was
naturally somewhat amused by the assumption that he could
learn from American ecumenical practices, which seemed
from his perspective to be "primitive." The fact is that there
is very much mutual mistrust and fear between the two
groups, partly derived from general causes and partly from
conditions that are uniquely American.

It should be recognized on both Protestant and Catholic
sides that religion can be a complicating factor in ethnic and
racial rivalries. An ethnically heterogeneous nation, such as
our own, will be impatient, therefore, with religious prejudices that aggravate ordinary points of tension. The tension
between Catholicism and Protestantism is largely a tension
between the Irish and the Anglo-Saxon in Boston, and be-

tween earlier and later migrations in the rest of the country, or sometimes between the Nordic and the Slav or Latin. Our religious institutions can assuage, rather than aggravate, these tensions only if there is knowledge of the peculiar force of the religious factor, and commerce rather than hostility between the religious communities.

Beyond this obvious cause there are other points of friction between us. To the Protestant, the Catholic Church will seem to be a political power rather than a religious community; and to the Catholic, the Protestant Churches will seem to be Christianity in various states of dissolution into secularism rather than Christian communities. There is no full justice in either impression, but these impressions are bound to grow in a situation of hostility. Naturally one wonders why we could not establish methods of intercourse through which Protestants might learn to appreciate the Catholic Church as a religious community with a treasure of graces of the spirit, and Catholics might know Protestant Churches as religious communities with a common treasury of faith rather than merely as rival political groups.

While the blame for a deplorable condition must be assessed fairly evenly between the two sides, I feel that Catholicism has a special blame on at least one point of friction between us. This point has to do with the effort to apply the standards of Natural Law to the life of the community. There is something ironic in the fact that the concept of Natural Law is regarded by Catholics as a meeting ground for Catholics and non-Catholics, and for Christians and non-Christians, whereas, as a matter of fact, it is really a source of tension between the Catholics and non-Catholics. Marital and family standards, on questions both of divorce and birth control, are the chief points at issue.

A Protestant Looks at Catholics

I remember participating in one of those formal symposia among Catholics, Jews, and Protestants that pass for serious discussion in America, in which the Catholic speaker blandly made the Reformation responsible for the moral relativism and nihilism that ends in "modern sexual promiscuity." It is one of the hazards of Catholic-Protestant relations (which require much more frank discussion to eliminate) that those of us who believe that rigid Natural Law concepts represent the intrusion of stoic or Aristotelian rationalism into the most dynamic ethic of Biblical religion are unqualifiedly accused of "moral relativism" or even moral nihilism: our motives in rejecting the thesis that a rigid legalism is the only cure for relativism are impugned; and we are given no credit for wrestling with the moral problems of such historical creatures as human beings who exhibit both a basic structure and endlessly unique elaborations of that structure. This in our opinion makes a rigid rational formula inapplicable while there is no situation in which the double love commandment is not applicable.

In regard to the problem of divorce, we do not, of course, challenge the right of the Church to preserve the Scriptural standard of the indissolubility of marriage in its community. But we believe it unwise to enforce this standard upon a semipagan or semisecular community by law, when as a matter of fact the preservation of marriage requires real grace and not merely the force of law. We believe that the secular State must do what Moses did "because of the hardness of your hearts," and we do not find the marital records of nations that prohibit divorce rigorously too impressive. They contain too many instances of clandestine arrangements outside of marriage.

The prohibition of birth control becomes a problem among

us when bishops threaten long-established "Community Chest" forms of communal co-operation because one of the charities included in the Chest may happen to harbor a birth-control clinic. The prohibition of contraception is regarded by some of us as an illustration of the fact that the Christian abhorhence of naturalism does not prevent Natural Law theories in this instance from sinking to a naturalistic dimension. Nothing is more obvious than the assertion that "nature" intends the end of procreation in sexual relations; but we believe also that the freedom of the human person rises indeterminately above the primary ends of nature. We believe that the temptation to abuse the new freedom which contraception makes possible is in no different category than the temptation and abuses in the whole of modern technical civilization.

The absence of genuine exchange of thought between Catholic and Protestant thinkers is particularly fruitful of misunderstanding on the question of Natural Law. I would myself like the opportunity to persuade Catholic friends that our failure to accept Natural Law theories does not mean that we are committed to moral relativism or even "nihilism." I would like to prove the honesty of our conviction that the "moral law," which Our Lord summarized in the double love commandment, is not to be equated with a "Natural Law" that is drawn from Stoic and Aristotelian conceptions. We question the seeming identification of "nature" and "reason" which Natural Law theories betray since early Stoicism. We feel that this identification rests upon the conviction that reality is "rational" in the sense that created things are related to each other by logical necessity. The Christian doctrine of creation by God's almighty act is contrary to this classical rationalism. We are baffled, furthermore, by the various ways in which "reason" is made into the source of law; and question the validity of each of the ways. Sometimes reason, by deductive process, seems to spin out the material content of law from the original proposition that we ought to do good and avoid evil. But we do not believe that the material content of ethics can be drawn from the formal principle of ethics. Sometimes it seems to be asserted that reason intuits specific moral propositions, thus bringing Natural Law proponents in harmony with the secular "moral sense" school of thought. The difficulty with this position is that there are undoubtedly universally valid and universally felt moral prohibitions. But they are most reliable and universal if they state minimal moral propositions such as the prohibition of murder or of incest.

But many supposedly "self-evident" propositions of more specific variety are dubious because they embody historically conditioned judgments and illicitly lift them to a dimension of unconditioned truth. Sometimes "reason" seems to function analytically in discerning the structures of "nature." There is undoubtedly a structure of human nature that must be discerned. There are things that "follow in a necessary manner from the fact that man is man" but the difficulty is that it is man's nature to transcend nature, including his own nature, indeterminately. In this freedom he elaborates a profusion of historical configurations in which essential human nature is compounded with contingent historical standards. In trying to find a universal principle under these shifting historical conditions, Natural Law proponents commit, in our opinion, one of two errors. They define the primordial, or even the purely biological, as normative, as for instance in the birth control issue, where "nature" is defined in purely biological terms. Or they mix some historically contingent standard with a perennial "natural" one. In the case of birth control it is

obvious that "nature" in the purely biological sense intends
sexual relations to have the end of procreation. But it is not
the "nature" of man merely to perpetuate himself; and a part-
nership between persons can and must have other ends than
procreation, even if that be its primary end in biological
dimensions.

It is significant that the second error operates to give contingent historical standards a false absoluteness. It was impossible, for instance, for medieval Christianity to grasp the historically contingent nature of a feudal-agrarian economy. It
was, therefore, inclined to defend its institutions as part of the
divine order against a rising bourgeois force. It was equally
impossible for the bourgeois secularists to notice the historically contingent aspects of what they defined as "nature's"
laws. Both types of theories failed to note that "God takes the
things that are not to put to naught the things that are."

We may go wrong in these our convictions about the validity of the Natural Law, but we find it an offense against Christian charity to be put into the camp of moral relativists by
our Catholic critics without any real debate between us.

The problem of religious education in our nation is a po-
tent source of friction and misunderstanding between the
Church on the one hand and Protestantism and the general
community on the other. Catholics may well be aggrieved to
find Protestants and secularists making common cause on this
issue and doing so upon the basis of a rigorous interpretation of the historic principle of the separation of Church and
State, which allegedly prohibits even the granting of auxiliary
services such as luncheons and bus rides to Catholic children.

Catholics know, and others ought to know, that this conception of an "absolute wall of separation" is not a *sine qua
non* of democracy as their opponents claim, because some

very healthy democracies in Europe do not observe a principle which our American "liberals" profess to regard as the cornerstone of democracy. Catholics have accepted the situation that forces them to pay double for their children's education with fairly good grace, knowing that whatever may be the tradition in other nations, the "secular" universal public school is a unique American institution that cannot be successfully challenged, not only because hallowed national traditions have a special potency but because the religious pluralism of our nation would make any other solution impossible. They are naturally baffled, and sometimes alarmed, when a nation that extols freedom endlessly seems to envisage the possibility of coercing attendance at the public school in the interest of national unity.

While causes of friction on this issue would seem to lie primarily on the Protestant side, and the Catholics rightly feel the force of a secularist-Protestant alliance against them, they probably do not appreciate the fact that their criticism of the secular character of the secular school is resented, particularly in view of the fact that they could not, in the light of their own principles, support a general religious instruction in the public schools. This resentment is hardly justified, however, since there could not be religious instruction in the public schools even without this complication.

Some of us who would like to see the State grant auxiliary services to Catholic children feel that the failure of Catholics to assure the nation that such a grant would not mean the opening wedge for further claims upon the State for support of parochial schools has a tendency to stiffen opposition to policies that seem to Catholics to represent simple justice. But our expectation of such promises is probably unreasonable, and indeed the promises might prove ineffective in dissipating Protestant opposition to such measures.

I must apologize for considering the problem of Catholic-Protestant relations rather than the exact theme the editor assigned to me. This was done because of a pressing personal concern about the absence of any genuine community between us, and the conviction that the inevitable frictions between religious groups and Churches will breed mistrust, fear, and even hatred if there is no effort to eliminate misunderstandings.

We owe it to our common Lord to heal the breach between us and to eliminate the scandal of our enmities, which threaten the common decencies and the good order of our country. We would be well advised to remember that the secularism which we pretend to abhor has at least one resource necessary for the health of a democratic community. It knows how to make pragmatic compromises in order to achieve harmony between seemingly incompatible positions, and Christian charity would accomplish the same end if Christians were humble enough to achieve the necessary charity.

Will Herberg

A JEW LOOKS
AT CATHOLICS

CATHOLICISM in America today stands at its highest point of prestige and spiritual power. It is not hard to see why this should be so in this country as elsewhere in the Western world. In an age when the vacuities of "rationalism" and unbelief have become so painfully evident, Catholicism presents the picture of a dynamic faith sure of itself and capable of preserving its substance and power despite elaborate institutionalism. In an age of spiritual chaos and disorientation, Catholicism stands forth as the keeper of an enduring tradition that has weathered the storms of the past and stands unshaken amidst the disasters of our time. In an age of social disintegration and the resurgence of every kind of narrow particularism, Catholicism speaks for and exemplifies a universalism transcending, though not negating, state and nation, culture and civilization. In an age disillusioned with the claims and pretensions of both individualism and collectivism, Catholicism is recognized as the long-time advocate of a "third way," a society built on Christian responsibility, the society defined in the papal encyclicals and the "social teachings" of the Church. Finally, in an age characterized by a total assault on the human spirit, Catholicism has distinguished itself as the "friend of man and of culture," to employ the expression of a well-known Protestant theologian.

The stand of the Church for the dignity of man, today so gravely threatened by the upsurge of demonic totalitarianism, has impressed itself on many a secularist thinker of our time and has won ungrudging tribute from men otherwise hostile to everything the Church represents. Nor should it be overlooked that the Church's intransigent opposition to Communism, in contrast to the confusion, vacillation, or worse, prevalent in so many Protestant groups, has had a profound effect on the American people, leading them to regard the Church as "on our side" in a way that would have been unthinkable not so many years ago.

All of these statements seem to me to be true and important, but what I want to do in these paragraphs is not simply to pay tribute to the Church, even where tribute is so manifestly due; it is my purpose rather, taking the above generalizations as to the Church's enhanced position for granted, to make some comments of a critical nature from the point of view of a believing Jew who is deeply concerned with religion in its relation to the social and cultural problems of our time. It is my hope that these comments will prove of some use in helping American Catholics see themselves as a friendly outsider sees them.

Perhaps because of the Catholic position on Natural Law, Catholics sometimes seem to forget that man's "natural" reason is both limited by his creatureliness and distorted by his sinful egocentricity. As a consequence, Catholic thinking in the social and cultural spheres is often too apt and too ready to make black-and-white distinctions and thereby to lapse into premature absolutisms. How easy it is for Catholics to write off a thinker such as John Dewey or Sidney Hook as "secularist" and "irreligious," without realizing that the secular thinker may sometimes serve the divine purpose in a way that is not given to the conventional believer.

On the other hand, the same tendency toward making black-and-white distinctions leads many a Catholic to give too ready and too total an endorsement to institutions and cultures that are on the "right" side. There is in much Catholic thinking what can only be called a certain optimism, a certain cheeriness even, a tendency to smile indulgently upon the world and pat it on the back; as a matter of fact a good case could be made out for the contention that today it is the Catholic who, in his enthusiasm for the natural powers of man, has quite unwittingly come to occupy the position vacated by the disillusioned votary of the liberal doctrine of progress. This may surprise those who tend to think of Catholics as gloomy ascetics absorbed in brooding over sin. These are not the Catholics I know, either personally or in their writings. Indeed, my criticism adds up to the charge that Catholics do not take sin and the human predicament resulting from sin seriously enough and therefore tend to overlook the profound ambiguity of all our thinking and doing.

Another way of phrasing this criticism, a characteristically "Jewish" way, is to say that in Catholicism, in this country at least, the "priestly" element is predominant, very much at the expense of the "prophetic." I mean, putting the matter a little too crudely perhaps, that there is too much cultivation of the traditional, the conventional, the regular, and too little readiness to break bounds and venture forth. Catholic thinking, by and large, is too much preoccupied with self-congratulation and self-justification and altogether too little concerned with self-criticism. There is not enough appreciation of the profound insight expressed in Reinhold Niebuhr's maxim relating to our social and political convictions: "We must fight their falsehood with our truth, but at the same time fight the falsehood in our own truth." This, it seems to me, is the true "prophetic" spirit, and it is this that I find lacking in much of American Catholicism.

On another level, the same tendency is expressed in the Catholic readiness to identify the Christian cause with the particular temporal interests of the Church. Such readiness shows little awareness of the perils and ambiguities of power, even where power is exercised in or by the Church. Examples of this tendency abound.

Catholicism does, of course, preach the doctrine of Original Sin, but in their own corporate life and practice American Catholics show too little sense of standing under the continuing judgment of God, which shatters all our pretensions and calls into question all our easy certainties and assurances. This would be my basic criticism of American Catholicism as I know it.

In contemporary American life, Catholicism plays a notably constructive role. It needs no proof, I think, that on labor and most social questions, American Catholicism is emphatically on the side of the angels. On the basic issue of Church and State, particularly in education, the Catholic position, Reinhold Niebuhr has testified, is "democratic in two senses of the term. It resists the claim of the state to enforce uniform education in the name of the right of parents to give their children an education according to their convictions. It is also democratic in the sense that a Christian viewpoint emphasizes the true dimensions of the individual, as having his ultimate authority and fulfilment above the political community and social process in which he is involved." (*Christianity and Crisis*, Feb. 2, 1953.)

A Jew Looks at Catholics

We may acknowledge this freely and gratefully, yet the question arises in the non-Catholic's mind—and it must be recognized as a very disturbing question—whether the liberal, democratic, pluralistic emphasis of Catholicism in America is for the Church a matter of basic principle or merely a passing counsel of expediency and necessity, motivated by its present minority status. Suppose Catholics were to become an overwhelming majority and non-Catholics "numerically insignificant" in this country, what then? Ryan and Millar, in their treatise *The State and the Church*, tell us in effect that in such a case Catholics would use their power to repeal the First Amendment, establish the Catholic Church as the State church, and outlaw free proselytizing activities on the part of non-Catholics, who would, however, be permitted religious practices "in the family or in such inconspicuous manner as to be an occasion neither of scandal nor of perversion to the faithful"! Is this to be taken as authoritative Catholic doctrine? American Jews, who prize the First Amendment as the charter of their freedom as a minority group, are very much concerned to know.

I know that recently there has been made a serious effort—I am thinking of Jacques Maritain and of the Jesuit, Father John Courtney Murray, among others—to restate Catholic doctrine in such a way as to make it quite unequivocal in its democratic-pluralist emphasis. I am much impressed with the thinking of these men, but do they speak for the Church? The violent opposition to Maritain in certain Catholic quarters is well known, and I myself have been warned on more than one occasion against the insidious influence of "Courtney Murrayism." In short, what *are* the long-range purposes and intentions of the Church in these matters so central to the

41

concern of every democratic American, particularly of every American Jew?

The question is rendered all the more urgent by the fact that Catholics in America as elsewhere have sometimes used the power that has fallen to them in certain localities in ways that have suggested the intention of enforcing Church doctrine and of making it binding on non-Catholics as well. The recent demand that the Welfare and Health Council of New York deny the affiliation of the Planned Parenthood Federation on pain of Catholic withdrawal may serve as an example; so too may the unhappy affair in Poughkeepsie, where non-Catholic doctors were dropped from a Catholic community hospital because of their membership in a birth-control group and were reinstated only after considerable public pressure. The Church has, of course, the full right to condemn contraception and to prohibit the faithful from resorting to it; but have Catholics the right, is it in conformity with the democratic ethos, to use their power, as they have in more than one state, to prevent non-Catholics from resorting to it?

Other examples come to mind, but they need not be recounted here. I am not suggesting that the American people anywhere are groaning under a Catholic despotism or that we are threatened with one; that would be nonsense. Nor am I singling out Catholics to condemn for misusing power; every group tends to misuse power to the degree that it possesses it without check, and that applies to Protestants, Jews, and secularists as well. What I am saying is that Catholic thought on the use of power by Catholics remains painfully ambiguous, and until that ambiguity is cleared up, the Catholic position in the American community will always in some sense remain a difficult one.

Equally serious, more serious indeed in its immediate consequences, is the practical secularism that pervades American Catholic life (no more, to be sure, than it pervades American Protestant or American Jewish life, but it is of Catholics that I am speaking here). It may seem strange to charge such doughty champions of religion as American Catholics with secularism, but what is secularism but the outlook in which religion is separated from life and relegated to a purely private status, peripheral to the vital areas of economics, politics, and culture, which are held to have autonomous nonreligious foundations? What is secularism, in short, but the conviction that "business is business," the affair of the businessman, just as "religion" is the affair of the priest? In this sense, secularism quite pervades the thinking of large numbers of American Catholics—a fact testified to by a familiar Catholic attitude that resents papal encyclicals on labor and industry as an intrusion of religion into a sphere where it does not properly belong.

The case of Joseph P. Ryan, the indicted president of the International Longshoremen's Association, is significant. Mr. Ryan is a Catholic and a trustee of the Guardian Angel Church in New York City. The pastor of the church is also port chaplain of New York. According to the press, not long ago he expressed his conception of the relation of religion to life in these words: "He [Mr. Ryan] keeps his hands off the spiritual things of my church and I keep my hands out of his business."

The same secularist doctrine has tended to obscure responsibility for political corruption and civic mismanagement perpetrated by "good" churchgoing Catholics; Boston, I should say, offers quite an object lesson. No one proposes that the Church directly intervene in politics or business or labor affairs, but it seems to me it ought not to be possible, as it manifestly is today, to be held a "good" Catholic without regard to what one does in one's business, political, or professional life. "Spiritual things" and "business" belong together, and when they are kept apart, it is "business," the common life, that is degraded, and the Church that is devaluated and discredited.

Because of this pervasive secularism, American Catholicism often allows itself to be caught up in the narrowness and petty prejudices of its environment. European observers, Catholic and non-Catholic alike, have marveled at the prudishness of American Catholics in matters of sex, an attitude so foreign to classical Catholic tradition. A good deal of this is probably an Irish heritage, but not entirely; the influence of American Protestant moralism is also a major factor. The slightest hint of sexual suggestiveness is pounced upon as the work of the devil, while movies, stories, and advertising that quite shamelessly strive to excite pride, envy, hate, and covetousness (sins rather high on the list) go by without a word of censure. Here American Catholics are most deplorably untrue to Catholicism.

I referred earlier to the tendency in Catholicism to smile indulgently upon men and pat them on the back, as it were. Catholicism thus comes forward as the friend of man, whereas Protestantism, with its unrelenting emphasis on judgment, sometimes appears as his enemy. But this same spiritual geniality, combined with the secularism to which I have alluded, often betrays Catholics into too easy an acquiescence in the banalities, timidities, and mediocrities of everyday life—provided they do not violate the conventional decencies. The utter mediocrity of so much of American Catholicism is to me a most shocking thing. How many times have I heard an intelligent and deeply sensitive Catholic say deprecatingly: "Oh, you can't expect too much of them; after all, they're only human . . ."—as if to be human meant to be commonplace and mediocre! Why is American Catholicism so uncreative, when compared with European? Why does it show so little appreciation of the great cultural treasures of its own tradition? There are many reasons, but I suggest that one of the most important is a deplorable readiness among many American Catholics of culture and intelligence to compromise with stupidity, stodginess, and mediocrity, so long as these keep within the bounds of "morality."

Mediocrity is reinforced by the tendency toward separatism and seclusiveness that is characteristic of much of American Catholic life. I refer not primarily to the vast network of special Catholic institutions and agencies, from academic associations and church schools to singing societies and sports clubs, which parallel the general community institutions; these mostly serve a useful purpose. What I have in mind rather is a kind of "secessionist" spirit that keeps the Catholic busy about his own Catholic affairs and leaves the business of the community, except politics, of course, largely to non-Catholics.

My university lecturing schedule and other interests brought me to a considerable number of cities and towns in various parts of the country during the past two years, and everywhere, I think, I found the same situation and heard the same complaints. "Oh, they're very nice," Protestants and Jews would say when I asked about the Catholics, "but they're never around; they keep to themselves and don't take part in things. They've got their own concerns. . . ." It is this same attitude, perhaps, that accounts for the strange indifference of so many Catholic educators to the problems of public education: their own special Catholic problems they feel they have solved, at least in principle, through the parochial school; the public school, even though it is attended by the great bulk of American children and Catholics are frequently quite influential in its administration, does not seem to strike them as a particular concern of theirs.

This feeling is undoubtedly in good part a carry-over from an earlier time when Catholics were indeed excluded from general community life; a good deal of it too may be traced to the logic inherent in the system of dual institutions that has been built up. But much of this attitude, it seems to me, is the indirect consequence of a deliberate policy of secluding Catholics in order to protect them from "contamination." I have heard this policy explicitly defended on more than one campus, though it is certainly not the rule at American colleges today. It seems to me unfortunate on all counts; it is utterly ineffective; it leads to a kind of social and intellectual isolationism that fosters narrowness and stagnation; and it is manifestly prejudicial to the position of Catholics in American life. Catholics are no longer aliens and outcasts in America; they have not been for some time—and they ought to cease acting as if they thought they were.

The criticisms I have made here are criticisms not of Catholic teaching but of attitudes and practices that seem to me to be essentially untrue to Catholic doctrine and tradition; as such, they have on occasion been made by Catholic critics themselves. They are made in good faith to help American Catholics see themselves as others see them and thus to enhance the possibilities of frank, openhearted co-operation among those who, as Christians or as Jews, serve the living God in the common cause and the common hope.

John J. Kane

CATHOLIC SEPARATISM

Do CATHOLIC institutions and organizations segregate American Catholics from the mainstream of the nation's life? Such a question is neither bigoted nor exaggerated. It has been raised recently by both Catholics and non-Catholics. While still at Harvard, James Conant criticized all private education as divisive. Some Catholic critics hold that Catholics tend to live in a cultural ghetto. Protestant publications have charged Catholics with perpetuating a cultural pluralism which they consider evil in a democratic society. The question is so compelling that the Catholic Bishops of America, assembled in their annual conference, considered it. Their statement, it is true, dealt mainly with Catholic schools, but the problem is more complex than this because the Catholic school system is only a part of Catholic separatism.

In the United States today, educational institutions under the sponsorship of Catholics range from nursery schools and kindergartens to graduate and professional schools in universities. There are Catholic orphanages, hospitals, social agencies, academic societies, fraternal orders, newspapers, magazines, labor and professional guilds, and war veterans associations. Catholics, however, are not unique in this respect.

47

Larger Protestant denominations and Jews operate hospitals, publish papers and periodicals, and maintain social agencies. There is a Jewish War Veterans group. There are Lutheran and Seventh-day Adventist parochial schools. If one stops here, one must conclude that all such activities are divisive or none are divisive. But the matter does not rest here.

Catholics are not only a religious group. They are also a "minority" group. Used in this sense, minority has no meaning in terms of numbers. It refers to the fact that some groups suffer discrimination at the hands of the majority. Jews, Catholics, Negroes, and foreigners are generally apt to fall into the minority classification in the United States. The sharpness and extent of discrimination differ with the various groups but all encounter it to some degree. Furthermore, minorities usually try to maintain their own culture in the face of an alien culture. One method for such preservation is a partial or wholesale withdrawal. The history of the Jewish people illustrates this point. Often forced into ghettos, compelled to wear distinctive dress, limited to certain occupations, Jews were thrown back upon themselves. A reinforcement of their culture followed.

Catholics are the largest minority in America. But the number and variety of their institutions and organizations cannot be explained solely on this basis. Catholic separatism results from at least three factors: historical accommodations in American life, severity of Catholic persecution by the majority group, and deep philosophical and religious differences with Protestantism and contemporary secularism.

To understand contemporary parallelisms of secular institutions by Catholics, it is necessary to gain some historical perspective. The ten years extending from about 1840 to 1850 significantly altered the development of Catholicism in the

United States. Until this decade American Catholics were mainly of English and French extraction. The Catholic hierarchy was largely French. Both had managed to live in peace within Protestant America. Then the most severe of periodic Irish famines sent thousands from southern Ireland to the United States.

These immigrants were a rural people. Their major occupation was farming, which meant that their past experience and skills were useless in an urban environment. Yet they settled in eastern seaboard cities, largely because of two factors. Acute poverty made it impossible for them to go West in search of cheap land, and attempts to settle Irish immigrants in the West usually met strong clerical opposition. It was feared that such dispersal would mean a loss of the faith because the few priests available could not minister to a scattered flock.

The southern Irish were overwhelmingly Catholic. Yet they settled in a Protestant country. These Irish immigrants came with empty stomachs as a result of famine, and empty purses as a result of poverty. But they brought with them a fear and hatred of things Protestant that had been engendered by centuries of persecution and attempted proselytizing by English Protestants. They brought with them a Catholicism that was an odd mixture of religion and nationalism. To be a Catholic was to be a true Irishman. To be an Irishman was to be a true Catholic.

With them came their native Irish clergy to sustain them spiritually and assist them temporally in the new world. For a long time some of these priests had opposed emigration because they feared it would mean a loss of the faith. In the face of famine they had to capitulate and themselves came to America to preserve the faith of the Catholic Irish.

Among Irish immigrants there was a dearth of lay leadership. With very few exceptions the only educated Irish in America were the clergy. Very soon they displaced the more temperate and less fearsome French hierarchy in America. Like members of their flock they were militant Catholics. Here they encountered a militant Protestantism. The two met head on.

Attacks were not long in coming, but here an important distinction is necessary. Were the attacks directed primarily at the Irish or at Catholicism? In a sense, perhaps, this distinction is a futile one. Irish and Catholic became so identified in American minds, as indeed they had earlier in Irish minds, that the mass of people could not differentiate between the two. Yet at the height of the Philadelphia riots, when Irish Catholic churches were burned to the ground, even though guarded by militia, a German Catholic church remained unguarded and unattacked although it stood within a few blocks of the actual rioting. It should also be remembered that by 1840 French and English Catholics appeared to have worked out a *modus vivendi* with their American Protestant neighbors. To what extent were the Irish, as Irish, to blame?

First, they came in large numbers. In the fifteen years after 1850, over seventy-five thousand Irish immigrants entered through the port of Philadelphia alone. In 1850 there were over seventy-two thousand foreign-born Irish in the County of Philadelphia. Within the city limits proper, one out of every five persons was Irish. Almost half of the Irish lived in the southwestern section of the city. In one ward they made up over 45 per cent of the population. For these reasons they were very visible. They clustered together, largely for economic reasons. Theirs were the most menial of jobs, and they lived close to the docks and freight yards where they worked. Their poverty reduced some of their areas to slums, which were cited as public nuisances.

At that time Philadelphia suffered periodic plagues, and popular concern over Irish living habits was intensified by this fact. Fraudulent nationalization methods enabled Irishmen to become citizens and voters almost at once. Tendency to vote one ticket was increased by density in certain wards, making the wardheeler's job an easy one. Rioting was common and not confined to the Irish, but they took part.

A stereotype was created that failed to include many sterling qualities of these new immigrants, but was not without some basis in fact. On many counts native Americans had reason for concern over the Irish influx, and the Philadelphia picture was repeated in most northeastern cities.

Regardless of these factors, however, religion became the focus of conflict. In the beginning, impoverished Irish Catholics had few schools, orphan asylums, or hospitals. To educate their children, to care for their sick and parentless, and to reform their wayward, they used whatever institutions existed. But whether such institutions were public or private, they were almost overwhelmingly Protestant. By 1840 the Protestant Orphan Society had a virtual monopoly over public education in New York City. It operated over one hundred schools and distributed over one hundred thirty thousand dollars annually, part of which was appropriated by the state common school fund. Ray Allen Billington writes in *The Protestant Crusade:* "Catholics had a just cause for complaint against this monopoly. The King James version of the Scriptures was read daily in all of the schools of the society and the regular prayers, singing and religious instruction were not in accord with Catholic belief. Particular

51

grounds for complaint existed in the textbooks used in the society's schools: all were blatantly Protestant in sympathy and many were openly disrespectful of Catholicism."

The *Catholic Herald* of Philadelphia charged that systematic kidnaping of Catholic children was occurring in the city. It cited the case of Arthur O'Neill, who had been arrested by the "beggar detectives" and turned over to the House of Refuge. This, the paper said, was part of a Protestant plot to proselytize Catholic children.

A month later this same paper stated that the Alms House, Girard College, and various homes for friendless children were really Protestant institutions. Prisons and penitentiaries were all anti-Catholic, the paper continued, and priests were not permitted to visit within their walls. It concluded: "Shall we stand tamely and idly by and permit the children of poor parents to be kidnaped in our streets, perverted in our schools, the aged proselytized in the Alms House and denied the ministrations of a priest in our hospitals?"

Catholics were further angered by refusal of officials to grant public funds for the institutions they did establish. The City Council of Philadelphia voted one thousand dollars for the Northern Home for Friendless Children, a Protestant institution, but refused to appropriate funds for a Catholic institution. Pressed for an explanation, the Council said that two-thirds of the money they voted for Protestant institutions went for relief of Catholics. Catholic sources did not deny this but protested that such institutions were used for proselytizing Catholic inmates. Attempts to have a Catholic version of the Bible read in public schools to Catholic children, as was done in Baltimore, resulted in rioting, bloodshed, and burning of Catholic churches in Philadelphia.

To preserve their faith and that of their children, the

poverty-stricken Irish immigrants had to set up what practically amounted to a set of parallel institutions. Once this method of accommodation was under way, it threatened to grow. In 1860 the Irish Catholic Benevolent Union was formed on a national scale. In the words of one ardent supporter who addressed the bishops and clergy of the United States: "Finally, it [the Irish Catholic Benevolent Union] is destined to become a power in the land, a power that becomes all the more necessary as the country is already inundated with unions, leagues, associations and secret societies that deprive many Catholics of the very means of sustenance."

Father John Hennessey, later Bishop of Wichita, envisioned a future in which the Irish Catholic Benevolent Union would have its own bank, an immigrant bank, to secure passage for immigrant families, an immigrant hotel to house them on arrival, agents to meet immigrants at wharves and railroad stations, and even their own steamships and employment offices. Even a separate Catholic labor movement came into being because the Knights of Labor were suspect in some Catholic quarters. Cardinal Gibbons intervened with Rome to prevent condemnation of the Knights of Labor, and the Catholic movement ended.

Behind the multiplication of Catholic institutions and organizations were two factors: preservation of the faith, and, later, hope of increased economic opportunities for Catholics, against whom discrimination was still strong. It required a critical situation to bring this parallel system about, but its own inertia could carry it on, even if later it served no great need. But in one sense the germs of its perpetuation were contained in the system. Not only was a Catholic culture preserved, but an Irish Catholic culture was preserved, as distinguished from German or Latin Catholicism. All, of course, are systems of belief in entire agreement with the body of faith and morals known as Roman Catholicism, but there are certain accidental differences.

Among the characteristics of Irish Catholicism is a tendency to Jansenism, a Catholic version of Puritanism. Jansenism was a French heresy, condemned by the Church. Irish priests, many of whom were educated in France, were influenced by this teaching, which they in turn passed on to their people.

Another characteristic of Irish Catholicism is an exaggerated reverence for the clergy, notably absent among most Latin Catholics. It was this which the English Catholic novelist Evelyn Waugh criticized when he visited the United States. For years most Irish Catholics had no education except that surreptitiously provided in "hedge schools" by clerical teachers. Priests were almost the only educated persons, and as such became leaders, not only in religion but in almost all matters. In a sense Irish Catholics tended to project onto all priests a sort of infallibility, and, unlike papal infallibility, it extended to all matters, sacred and profane.

Lastly, Irish Catholicism was interwoven with nationalism. Hope for the freedom of Ireland was second only to the hope of eternal salvation. This nationalism involved a hatred of all things English and Protestant, and little distinction was made between the two. In establishing Irish Catholic institutions and organizations to preserve the faith, and later to offset anti-Catholic discrimination, Irish Catholics, perhaps unwittingly, preserved strong elements of this nationalism. Such attitudes were not conducive to co-operation with Protestants, even in matters not involving religion.

In the past, separatism was an effective method of transmitting and preserving the faith. An Irish Catholic of the last century might well have lived his life and satisfied most of his needs within a Catholic ghetto. Economic adjustment, however, required daily excursions into a Protestant or secular society. Over the years, this narrow gap in the wall has been widened as Catholics have achieved some measure of "vertical mobility."

Today Catholics no longer huddle together in certain sections of a city. City parishes are large and contain diverse elements of the Catholic population. The bonds of nationalism, once helping to cement the parish, have been weakened or obliterated. About half the Catholic children attend nonparochial schools. Mixed marriages appear to be increasing. Some Catholic societies lead a precarious existence in terms of interest and support.

In the past, Catholic schools were certainly an effective bulwark of the faith, but today all schools face serious competition with more elaborate and widespread media of communication. Newspapers and magazines have tremendous circulations. Radio and especially television are methods of education that reach more and more people, and reach them during most hours of the day and night. Finally, motion pictures, although perhaps declining in influence, have been and still are an excellent means of communicating ideas. Most of these media not only eschew any denominational line, but tend to be secularistic.

Nor have the consequences of Catholic separatism been entirely satisfactory. True, Catholicism has been preserved. Every wave of Catholic immigration has found well-established institutions ready to serve it and help it preserve the faith. But Catholic influences on American life have been much less than a Catholic population of almost thirty million might have been expected to make. Furthermore, a great deal of it has been negative. Too frequently it has taken the form of protests, picketing of theaters, voting against legislation without pressing for alternative measures to solve problems. So often Catholic attitudes have been all black or white without distinguishing the neutral grays. Mussolini was a great man because he signed a concordat with the Vatican. Franco is highly acceptable because he does not persecute Catholics. Child-labor legislation is opposed because it may threaten the natural rights of parents. All Catholics, of course, have not shared such opinions, but an impression to that effect has been created.

Non-Catholics are almost entirely unaware of the freedom of thought that does exist in Catholicism. There are matters of faith and morals on which complete acceptance is demanded. There are matters so closely related to faith and morals that prudence persuades acceptance. But beyond these are many areas in which no such thing as unanimity of Catholic opinion exists.

Two conclusions can now be drawn: Catholic separatism, as reflected in a set of parallel institutions, has lost much of its effectiveness in the contemporary world. Its future appears even more dismal.

The increased birth rate following the war is taxing the resources of parochial education. There is some evidence that vocations to the religious life, particularly to sisterhoods, have not maintained an increase proportionate to the population. Lay teachers are expensive, and for a century parochial education has been possible because of vows of poverty taken by the teaching orders.

In higher education, prospects are worse. Few Catholic colleges and universities have endowments; those that do find them meager by comparison with nonsectarian schools.

Catholic Separatism

The cost of equipment, especially scientific laboratories, is tremendous. State aid appears unlikely, and the future of small Catholic colleges is in jeopardy. It seems almost inevitable that a large proportion of Catholic college students will be educated in private, nonsectarian, or state universities. Here is a challenge twentieth-century Catholicism must prepare to meet.

Catholic separatism tends to lessen or limit Catholic participation in, and influence on, some aspects of American life. The wall of separatism effectively staved off a militant Protestantism of the last century. It will not defend against an equally militant secularism of the twentieth century. In fact, the wall of separatism has already been breached, and its repair appears doubtful.

The indicated stratagem is a sally. Furthermore, it should be remembered that there are allies outside the wall among religious-minded persons of all faiths. Grave differences separate these allies from each other and from Catholics. But all can join on the basis of what they do share in common without compromising differences. This, it appears, must supplant the American Catholic accommodation of separatism.

Joseph M. Duffy, Jr.

CLERGY AND LAITY

Some months ago the New York *Times* gave quite extensive coverage to a talk by a priest that I would like to make use of here. I am interested in the talk, not because of its occasion, a Communion breakfast, nor because of its author, whom I have no particular desire to criticize, but because its point of view provides such a convenient springboard for the subject at hand. My subject is clergy and laity, and the things I will say have to do mainly with the negative aspects of the relations between the clergy and the laity in this country—the climate of drought, if you will, instead of the fertile season.

The speaker declared that the Church in the United States was seriously threatened by a shortage of priests. This situation, he maintained, has been brought about, on the one hand, by the prevalence of Catholic "birth controllers" and, on the other, by a "secret" Communist plot to subvert the Church by dividing the laity from the hierarchy.

Elaborating on the second danger, he asserted that Communists have joined the Church in order to criticize it from within and he claimed that some Catholic writers, by their criticism of the clergy, have followed the "Communist campaign." Sean O'Faolain was singled out for his *Life* article on Ireland, and Thomas Sugrue for his book, *A Catholic Speaks His Mind.*

These writers and their works are of little concern here. The most damning fact about Mr. O'Faolain's article, which was serious and interesting, was that it appeared in a March 16 issue of *Life:* that impresses one as a gesture of gratuitous impertinence of the kind that Luce publications have always enjoyed making. Beyond that, most of us realize that Ireland is one of two taboo travel subjects—Spain is the other— among certain articulate segments of the American Church: taboo, that is, unless the writer is prepared to accept history as it has been scrupulously rewritten in these quarters. Of Mr. Sugrue, about whose writings it is difficult not to have some reservations, one can at least invoke the charitable banality, *"De mortuis. . . ."*

What *is* of central concern here, however, is that the talk was both a confession of failure and an admission of diffidence. It prefigures the large failure and the larger diffidence that I wish to comment on. The sin of the laity—the "unbelievable" number of Catholic "birth controllers"—is the failure of the clergy. (I do not mean to shift the responsibility here, merely to indicate a failure of influence.) And the warning against Communist infiltration of the Church surely betokens not so much a fear of Communism as a fear of criticism.

Last year a much more prominent clergyman, who has opinions on many subjects, issued a similar warning. In spite of the real case of Father Tondi, the Italian Jesuit who left his order to join the Communists, one cannot help perceiving that this cautious advice may be strategically turned against any evaluation of the clerical position, however sincere and upright the evaluation may be. A statement of this kind provides a frame to distort all criticism; it prepares the way for clerical McCarthyism; it looks for orthodoxy and conformity in areas where these attributes are not desirable. The failure, the sin, and the diffidence are, so to speak, the bones one falls upon in the drought.

In his pastoral letter, *Priests among Men,* Cardinal Suhard, the late Archbishop of Paris, states that "a priestless society is a dead society, a civilization which neither makes sense nor achieves anything." The priest, Cardinal Suhard reminds us, "must not be set in opposition to the faithful as though the latter had nothing in common with him"; yet he is also "a man set apart from the faithful, endowed by God with transcendent powers and marked with a consecratory character which sets him apart, makes him at once pontiff and head in the community of the baptized."

Cardinal Suhard describes the "counterfeits" of the priest, the false images that are created of him—those of angel, wonder worker, and superman. Moreover, Cardinal Suhard warns, false expectations are raised about the role of the priest in the social order: by some he is wrongly thought of as the conservator of the old order, and by others he is just as wrongly looked to as the prophet of the new.

Cardinal Suhard's letter deserves wide circulation—there is much more in it about the function of the priesthood and about the reciprocal duties of the clergy and the laity. I find great reassurance and strength in his emphasis upon the necessity for a priesthood if our civilization is to survive.

In an age of secularism, the priesthood is paradoxically a source of order to the faithful and of bewilderment to the secularists; the priesthood is a challenge and reproach to the bland inanity of secularism, whose principles are joyless, cruel, and, in the long run, authoritarian. If the poets, as

Allen Tate says in *The Forlorn Demon,* are the prophetic demons in a secularist society, reminding it of the hell wherein it exists, the priesthood is the instrument of salvation, the anodyne for the barren torment.

Consequently I admit the difficulty of criticism. When I consider the heroic examples of clerical action under diverse circumstances, in war and peace, amid danger abroad and exhaustion at home, among the workers, the alienated, and the dispossessed, and among the comfortable, the respectable, and the indifferent; when I consider the unknown lives of the unknown clergymen, dully passed in the quotidian routine that is transformed by their dedication into a routine of love, so much more difficult, nobler in a sense, than the heroic gesture, the grand and startling deed; and when I consider the rich and joyful lives of those I have known among the clergy and laity whose joy comes from their privileged membership in the community of the Church, I almost believe that criticism is supererogatory and always inopportune. But the actual is large, complex, and portentous: too large and complex to be settled by a panegyric, and portentous in its examples of indifference, timidity, and failure.

In the life of the Church, and by that I mean the corporate activity of all its members, the culture of our time may be mocked. In America we live in an externalized society where individuals pass disconsolate lives devouring the material and transient object; its members, passionately adrift, lured by slogans and pricked by greed, always fail to achieve the promised satisfaction in the object.

At its weakest, ours is a culture of commodities where the lust for things is never met even by an endless production of things, where new desires are daily provoked and new standards of conformity daily imposed. Indeed, the Platonic ideal of our system, the heroic figure dimly perceived by the advertising people from their caves, is the insatiable consumer who never dies and who will exhaust an eternity of production in his effort to attain comfort, health, and modishness.

As Catholics we have a special status in this society; we are of it and partake of its advantages, which are real and good and not to be rejected, but we also have the power of making distinctions at precisely those points where society fails to distinguish or cannot give ultimate reasons for its distinctions. We carry with us always a sense of mortality, the token of our mortality. We love one another as members of Christ's Mystical Body. And we respect the freedom of the individual as superior to all human institutions.

Do we? Often we are proud of our status and flaunt it before others. We attend the ritual, trace the formalistic pattern, and fail to observe the responsibilities of status. Often we do not love, we hate. We hate by omitting to love, and sometimes, as happened last year in a marginal Puerto Rican district in New York, our sins of omission are symbolically transformed by a senseless and violent act of hatred perpetrated, as in this case, by Catholics upon Catholics.

Often we are attached to form without comprehension of the living attributes that make the form meaningful. We attend Mass on Sundays and view, amid flickering candles and the haze of incense, the richly vested figure who murmurs a strange language and engages in a half-understood ritual; rarely does the shock of realization disturb the memory of yesterday's business and today's pleasure.

Moderation, regularity, vague commitment descend to complacency and inertia and sink at last to the indifference that accounts for the scandalous divergency between doctrine and practice implied in the "unbelievable" number of Catholic "birth controllers." We are charmed by the myths of our society, acquire its prejudices, absorb its slogans, cherish its comforts, and languish in its mediocrity.

Our inconsistencies in these matters, our failure and our sin, dramatize the tension between the doctrine of the Church and the allurements of the world. Realistically viewed, they represent the enduring hardship of the human condition. Nevertheless, in every age we must renew the struggle to diminish these inconsistencies. Of crucial importance now and in this country, the extremes of the laity as otiose and tax-paying observers and the clergy as pious and platitudinous bureaucrats are the specters to be dissipated. Faith, doctrine, dogma, ritual, and action—all ought to involve us in a charismatic community of mutual understanding and participation.

If, however, the ideal among Catholics is, at one level, this community shaped by common doctrine and common aspirations, at another level we are as diverse in our thinking, pluralistic in our ideas, as any other group in our society. At least, that, too, is the ideal. But there are those within the Church who would compel formalism in nondoctrinal matters, who would freeze Catholic opinion in this country by maintaining that there is nothing in life so complex that it cannot be successfully tested by *their* measure of what is "Catholic" and what is not.

Sound and fury are the tactics commonly used to enforce these inflexible and self-styled "Catholic" standards. To a considerable extent the strategy has been successful: an imposing monolithic "no-nonsense" façade of clergy and laity does exist and does effectively shut out, for those within, the undistorted facts of life.

The ramparts are manned by the Catholic press, by our pulpits indeed, and by clerical-inspired vigilante groups among the laity who level wildly indiscriminate barrages at the camp of the enemy. The enemy may be real enough at times, but he frequently is just anyone "out there," anyone who displays alarming signs of nonconformity—a "leftist," for example, an intellectual, or an artist.

When we recall the history of the American Church's struggle for recognition under the most exasperating circumstances, we can understand the existence of scars that are still painfully sensitive. And the continuing hostility of certain groups and individuals who willfully misconstrue and libel the doctrines and motives of Catholicism is sufficiently abrasive to provide forthright response from the representatives of the Church.

When the occasion demands wrath, politeness is no substitute for just wrath. When a Protestant clergyman venomously refers to "Rome" as though he perceived the Whore of Babylon all decadent and lascivious before him, or when a "liberal" magazine insolently announces the selection of Mr. Paul Blanshard as its Holy Year correspondent in Rome, the challenge should be justly and vigorously countered.

But what can be neither understood nor accepted is the perpetuation of the ghetto attitude among Catholics. This attitude, nervous, irritable, and often absurd, simplifies and parodies life into an impossible choice of absolutes. In spite of the energy it manifests, this attitude of sullen exclusiveness is a sign, not of liveliness but of its opposite. When it unites the clergy and laity, it joins them in their weakness, ignorance, and complacency. Some examples of what I take to be the ghetto attitude may clarify these statements.

Several years ago, the newspaper of one of our great metropolitan dioceses denounced in an editorial a revival of *The Duchess of Malfi*. The editorial discovered in the production of the play convincing proof of an anti-Catholic plot in the commercial theater. Apparently it had not occurred to the editorial writer, for whom the wicked Cardinal loomed all imposing, that less sinister considerations might have motivated the revival of one of the handful of great English tragedies outside of Shakespeare.

Astonishing as it seems, and possibly more annoying to some than conspiracy, the producers of the play may not even have considered Catholic sentiment—may have been interested only in putting on an important dramatic work. If the line of the editorial's logic were followed, Chaucer could be rejected by Catholics because of his depiction of corrupt clergymen—as well as for his immorality—and by Jews because of the anti-Semitic basis of the Prioress's Tale.

The examples of such reasoning could be multiplied indefinitely. The murky, plot-filled world of the editorial writer simply is not the real world, and to present it as such to readers is to leave them in a condition of perilous innocence.

In *The Art of Fiction,* Henry James, referring to the situation in Victorian England, noted as a "Protestant" characteristic the suspicion of all artistic effort that was not clearly designed either to amuse or to edify. Curiously enough, this "Protestant" attitude is, in the United States, too often the "Catholic" attitude.

In this suspicion of art as such—which is a form of a prevailing anti-intellectualism, a widespread affinity for the mediocre—lies the danger of clerical attempts to enforce censorship by the provocation of boycotts and vigilante activity. Unable to make the complex distinctions required before an artistic or intellectual work is rejected, the suspicious authority stifles truth by acting indiscriminately.

The parish priest or the editor of a diocesan newspaper

may be competent to advise the laity about such works; but as events in this country have shown and as the present situation in Ireland certainly demonstrates, he may become dangerous when he attempts to enforce this advice through action. So, too, he may mislead the laity by recommending vulgar and pernicious works simply because they have a contrived aura of piety about them.

The motion picture "My Son John" was appropriately condemned by some Catholic critics and by secular reviewers who recognized it as a very dangerous picture indeed in its sophisticated and deliberate attack upon intellectual values. Yet it was widely praised in the Catholic press and received a Catholic award. The shocking simplicity of the "Catholic" response—sometimes the willingness to be duped seems like a fatality—may be explained by the exaltation in the picture of the pieties of the Church, Motherhood, the Nation, and the Playing Field. The quality of that exaltation and its implications were not questioned—the formal obeisance sufficed.

In the Catholic reaction to non-Catholic higher education in the United States, similar reservations must be made about a latent distrust of intellectual distinction. Among the American clergy and consequently among the laity, a tradition of profound discourtesy toward these colleges and universities predominates.

The grave faults of secular education warrant exposure, for they constitute the danger of residence at such institutions: the boundless confidence in the power of the intellect, the totemistic exaltation of freedom without any sense of controlling responsibility, the bland presentation of intolerant opinion as historical fact. But these same colleges and universities are also populated by individuals engaged in a quest for truth, whether their specialty be in art, science, or society.

Devotion to this ideal is a natural virtue, and to regard these men with supercilious condescension or to subject them to slanderous attacks, as spokesmen for the Church have done, has had results so intolerable that the time for reform is long past due. The unjustified complacency thus encouraged among Catholics about their own institutions and the unhealthy cynicism toward others have been rightly interpreted as tokens not merely of Philistinism but of Pharisaism.

Not long ago, a prominent Catholic clergyman and well-known educator referred in a speech reported in the New York *Times* to a recent problem in the educational world—that of a "fifth column," a "crop of starry-eyed liberals on the American campus" who could not distinguish between American inconsistencies and Russian barbarities. According to the educator, now in a whimsical mood, vodka disappeared from the faculty clubs after the Korean war and after the "distinguished" Senator from Wisconsin had "made pink unpopular." There is enough truth in a statement of this kind to make it plausible to a sympathetic and inexperienced audience, but the entire picture is palpably false.

A comparable charge against Catholic institutions would be that they are or have been inhabited by totalitarians who pay lip service to American principles but whose objective is the establishment of a Catholic authoritarian state. Such an accusation, were it made, would be justly ridiculed by Catholics. What is disturbing, then, is the incorrigible absence on the Catholic side of the merest courtesy toward institutions, the best of which, the best members of which, are simply engaged in the long labor of extending the horizons of human knowledge.

Furthermore, the reference to Senator McCarthy in this talk provides a grimly ironic parallel to the Communist fellow traveling here criticized. Unfortunately it is a parallel not unique in Catholic circles. Yet Catholics, clergymen least of all, should hardly submit to the general American infatuation with a perverted idea of innocence, an ideal of an earthly paradise swept bare of discordant elements. The clean sweep, it is clear, is to be made at the expense of values which, if they make life most difficult, also make it most dear.

McCarthy has not made pink unpopular; he has abandoned the spectrum and preserved only black and white. What the adventurer McCarthy promises—what all utopians, good and bad, in our national history have promised—is release from the almost unbearable complexities of the real world into a limbo of shining white American innocence where responsibility ceases.

But the dream, like the Marxist illusion of the '30s, inevitably turns out to be a nightmare conjured up by a charlatan. That Catholics do not recognize this temptation for what it is, when they can identify the temptation of the Marxists, means that they too have acquiesced to the delusion of bleak absolutes and have become wayfarers embarked on a pilgrimage to a blighted Arcady.

Returning to the Communion breakfast talk with which this essay began, I would directly reverse its proposition that criticism from within endangers the Church in the United States and say that criticism may well be an indication of the toughness of the living fiber, while inert acceptance of the clerical attitude in all matters may be evidence of fossilization. Naturally I am talking here not of criticism that rises out of rancor and is shaped by arrogance, but of the judicious assessment that is directed toward reconstruction and revival.

In a pluralistic society like our own, such criticism must

be warily offered lest it be misinterpreted and exploited by those outside the Church. In this day, we are deprived of the satisfaction Dante must have felt in populating the circles of the *Inferno* with notable examples of remiss clergy. But we still have the obligation—not merely the privilege—of pointing out, say, the perilous road being taken by Catholic fellow travelers of McCarthy.

Even at the risk of unpleasantness—that is, the risk of having one's religion, ancestral origins, and ability impugned—it is necessary to say frankly, when it seems to be the case, that the Catholic clergy and laity are not well-informed in many matters, are not equipped to deal with some of the problems they raise, and are not altogether candid in their appraisal of themselves and others. Having said so much among ourselves, we may discover some of the immense possibilities for growth through self-knowledge.

What we need to find again, possibly, are daring and foolishness. Satan, I suspect, finds dry rot a far more effective destroyer of souls than the heartbreaking temptation.

I am reminded here of a recent conversation with a priest during which he responded with mingled contempt and alarm to a reference to the Catholic Action movement in France. I realized that, for him, these French Catholics belonged in somewhat the same category as French novels. Only with the novels one knew, at least, what one had and could cast them out. With the Catholics one could not be sure. They appeared to resemble the familiar product, but they also had strange and upsetting ideas about the *status quo*.

Yet what is the merit of our lives, after all, if we do not dare disturb the established order with our love, joy, sacrifice, and belief? For these are the commodities our society, in all its wastefulness, has found too expensive to carry. United and diverse, as Catholics we can be, I trust, genuinely "subversive" elements on the American scene. By becoming what we can be, we have a job to do in our time.

John Cogley

CATHOLICS AND
AMERICAN DEMOCRACY

AMERICAN Jews live in a nation which solemnly and
joyously celebrates the birth of Christ every winter.
Seventh-day Adventists form part of a civil society which
almost universally accepts Sunday as the Lord's Day. Christian Scientists pay taxes to a government which subsidizes
medical programs solidly based on the germ theory of contagion. Biblical pacifists in the United States have to work
out their salvation in a nation which spends a shockingly
high percentage of its income on weapons of mass destruction. All these groups are, to some extent, "different." In a
pluralist culture like ours certain frictions and compromises
are inevitable.

Catholics, too, are "different." Whereas, for instance, most
Americans endorse the classical Protestant belief in private
judgment, we frankly profess our faith in, and offer our obedience to, an authoritarian Church. Whereas dogma is widely
regarded as being unworthy of an American's proud independence of mind, Catholics cheerfully accept the religious
doctrines and moral precepts of their Church as infallibly
true and binding in conscience. Whereas most Americans
subscribe to the idea that religion is a wholly private matter,

73

the Catholic publicly proclaims his belief in an unchanging Natural Law to which not only Catholics themselves but all men are bound. In a nation where it is a bromide that all religious paths lead to God and in the last analysis one Church is just about as good as another, Catholics say baldly that theirs is the only true faith, eternally right, and all others are more or less false.

These are only a few instances where Catholics are "different." If the area of difference were as narrow as that setting off Christian Scientists or Seventh-day Adventists, Catholics might merely be deemed eccentric. Or if we were as few in number as the Biblical pacifists, we might be treated, as they are, with benign tolerance. Or if we were as withdrawn as the single-minded sects which, in their search for heaven on earth, have cut themselves off from the steady stream of national life, we might go generally unnoticed. But Catholics in American life are numerous, well-organized, and politically active. There is a growing feeling that we are too numerous, too well-organized, and that Catholic political power is potential dynamite. It would be highly unrealistic, in any discussion of Catholics and American democracy, not to take this feeling—if that is not too mild a word—into account.

Suspicions and fears about Catholics are largely concerned not so much with the present as with the future—with what will happen on that improbable day when Catholics as a majority in the United States have the legal power to destroy the democratic way of life as it is now understood among us and to erect the classical "Catholic State" in this country.

In this "Catholic" America, it is fearfully anticipated, separation of Church and State will go; "error will have no rights" (that is, non-Catholic sects and churches will suffer severe

74

legal disabilities, losing, for instance, their present civil right to worship publicly and proselytize freely). Further, it is believed, many traditional liberties (freedom of press, of speech, and of academic procedure, for example) will be severely curtailed if not altogether abolished; the public expression of ideas "dangerous" or unorthodox from the Catholic viewpoint will be forbidden, and the laws of the land will be recast to conform rigidly to Catholic doctrine.

Very few critics of Catholicism actually believe that the Pope will move into the White House or even that he will take a very direct part in the internal affairs of a "Catholic" United States—which, I suppose, is progress of a sort; but the picture here drawn of a "Catholicized" nation surely haunts many discussions of Catholicism and American democracy. For instance, I suspect some such picture was in the minds of the Reverend Robert J. McCracken's parishioners when they heard their minister say from the pulpit of the Riverside Church, in 1951: "Roman Catholicism is engaged in a ceaseless surreptitious pressure to obtain a position of preference in the New World. Nor can there be any doubts as to the success attending its efforts."

It is, in short, the Catholic theory as they understand it that frightens non-Catholic Americans, more than the Church as it actually exists and operates in our national life. By the same token, whenever the popes have spoken of the actual conditions of American life, their words have been full of praise and commendation. Whatever restrictions are to be found in papal approval have also been on the level of theory. Thus in 1895 Pope Leo XIII, in his encyclical on Catholicism in the United States, *Longinque Oceani*, wrote these much-quoted words, which have been cited through the years to prove that the Catholic Church is not really satisfied with things as they are in the U.S. and would change basic American institutions if it ever gained the power to do so:

Moreover—a fact which it gives great pleasure to acknowledge—thanks are due [for the healthy state of the Church in the United States] to the equity of the laws which prevail in America and to the customs of that well-ordered Republic. For the Church among you, unopposed by the Constitution and government of your nation, is fettered by no hostile legislation, is protected against violence by the common laws and the impartiality of the tribunals, and is free to live and act without hindrance.

Yet though all this is true, it would be very erroneous to draw the conclusion that in America is to be sought the type of the most desirable status of the Church, or that it would be universally lawful or expedient for State and Church to be as in America, dissevered and divorced.

The fact that Catholicity is with you in good condition, nay, it is enjoying a prosperous growth, is by all means to be attributed to the fecundity with which God has endowed His Church, in virtue of which, unless men or circumstances interfere, she spontaneously expands and propagates herself; but she would bring forth more abundant fruits if, in addition to liberty, she enjoyed the favor of the laws and the patronage of the public authority.

Another quotation widely circulated in non-Catholic circles is taken from *Catholic Principles of Politics* (1940), written by two American priests, John A. Ryan and Francis J. Boland. This book, which is a revision of an earlier work by Monsignor Ryan and Morehouse F. X. Millar, an eminent Jesuit, dealt—in a famous passage—with a "Catholic State" and what it would mean if the United States were to become such a state. (It should be noted that an essential note of such a theoretical state is that its citizenry must be *overwhelmingly* Roman Catholic: the simple majority envisioned in many non-Catholic nightmares would not suffice.)

Catholics and American Democracy

Suppose that the constitutional obstacle to proscription of non-Catholics has been legitimately removed and they themselves have become numerically insignificant: What then would be the proper course of action for a Catholic State? Apparently the latter State could logically tolerate only such religious activities as were confined to the members of the dissenting group. It could not permit them to carry on general propaganda nor accord their organization certain privileges that had formerly been extended to all religious corporations, for example, exemption from taxation.

While all this is true in logic and in theory, the event of its practical realization in any State or country is so remote in time and in probability that no practical man will let it disturb his equanimity or affect his attitude toward those who differ from him in religious faith.

But, as the Reverend Robert McAfee Brown, a Presbyterian minister, put it in a recent letter to *The Commonweal,* "it *does* disturb our equanimity." In fact, Catholic statements like this "scare the living daylights out of Protestants."

Practically everyone, I think, will agree that the *probability* of a United States so changed that non-Catholics have become "numerically insignificant" is indeed remote. Still, I don't think it is the actual anticipation of a "Catholic State" that disturbs non-Catholics so much as the knowledge that a significant number of their fellow citizens entertain theories—even highly abstract theories—which, under certain circumstances, would justify the destruction of richly prized civil rights. "How," they ask, "can these people call themselves Americans? Ultimately, they don't believe in what America stands for." Their dismay is somewhat the same as that of Catholics themselves when they hear grandiose soapbox plans for America and the Church "come the revolution."

It is this basic uncertainty about Catholicism that underlies much non-Catholic suspicion in the United States. Many Americans, having only a hazy notion of the "Catholic State" theory, actually believe that the day American Catholics achieve a simple majority they will be ordered to press for its realization. And in the light of this, naturally enough, every Catholic excursion into public life is mistaken for "denominational aggression." The claim that parochial-school children have a right to ride in buses for which their parents have been taxed, for instance, is judged not on its own merits but, in a larger context, as the first step toward winning State support for Catholic schools. This in turn is seen as part of an over-all plan to "Catholicize" the United States—to make the textbook "Catholic State" a reality on American soil.

In such an atmosphere, every day becomes a possible D-day; the most innocent public statements of the Catholic hierarchy are invested with bellicose meanings; and otherwise benign and tolerant Americans turn into trigger-happy defenders of a liberty that is never truly attacked. The whole situation, especially during recent years, has been shrewdly exploited by enemies of Catholicism; it makes life difficult for the friends of the Church; and American Catholics themselves, sensing the general hostile atmosphere, often grow mindlessly defiant and trying—aggressive in manner if not in intent—like small boys who feel that they have been unjustly accused.

Ironically enough, the idea of a "Catholic State" is probably much more real to those who fear it than it is even to those doughty American Catholic apologists and writers who regularly come to its defense as an abstract, "logical" proposition, with what must surely be taken as a suspicious zeal. There is, alas, an unhappy ambiguity in the position of Cath-

78

olic theorists who are hurt and offended by the idea that other Americans deem Catholicism a threat to their own religious liberty, but who will yet clearly imply, by support of the "Catholic State" idea and justification of religious intolerance abroad, that the non-Catholic has solid reasons to be fearful. We can't have it both ways. However logical the case for Catholic intolerance, it is not a logic that moves the minds of those who see themselves as its potential victims.

Catholic "logicians" have sometimes been heard to argue that while we are in the minority we will live by *your* logic, the logic of tolerance, but when you are in the minority, you will have to live by ours. But if that be the game, one should be willing to pay its penalties, and the present atmosphere of suspicion and distrust would seem to be a cheap enough price. Logic, after all, is a two-way street.

For all that, I seriously doubt that any more than a few extremists, even among the ardent defenders of the "Catholic State" thesis, seriously envision, or would actually welcome, such a state on American soil. This is not very "logical" for such stern logicians, I agree, and probably seems highly incredible to one who does not know the American Catholic milieu. Understandably, the cold zeal with which Catholic students of philosophy and theology habitually deal with abstract propositions leads many to believe that they are as heartlessly "logical" in the world of affairs as in the realm of ideas. But, fortunately, this is rarely so. I have heard kindly, patient professors and even gentle nuns, for instance, defend the "logic" of the most frightful inquisitions; yet their personal lives clearly belied all their ferocious principles.

To the Catholic, who believes that Christ was God and that He founded a Church and remains with it, nothing is more obvious *as an abstract proposition* than that this Church is the only one that has a *logical* claim on the spiritual loyalty of mankind. For the Catholic to hold otherwise would involve either denying his faith in the uniqueness of the Church or doing violence to reason itself.

If no human beings were involved and the question did not come up outside the vacuum of a philosophy class, the matter could end there. But because the ideal (all men united in one true Church) does not conform to the real world (men, even Christian men, divided in their loyalty to many churches, each making its claims on the consciences of its adherents) the picture is radically changed. Still the fact that a religiously divided world unquestionably does exist in no way alters the doctrine that the one true Church has an abstract right to claim unique recognition.

All this, however, does not mean that such a claim would be pressed without consideration for a people's history, their national tradition and native temperament, or that it would be pursued at the cost of upsetting the whole political order under which the Church flourished before it gained the overwhelming majority that made its supposed ascendancy possible. An ideal relationship between Church and State presupposes an "ideal," textbook State.

Another writer once wrote in *The Commonweal:* "The guaranty of religious freedom which finally gained place in the Constitution of this country was no child of logic. It was derived from historical understanding. But the gains made by historical understanding should be no less permanent than those achieved in the natural sciences. It is just as important that men should believe in the doctrine of religious freedom as it is that they should believe the earth is round. As the modern geographic idea on the shape of the earth adjusts itself to real fact, so also religious freedom, including the right to worship as one chooses and to propagate what one believes to be religious truth, adjusts itself to the historical facts of human life, thought and experience." (*"On Modern Intolerance,"* by James N. Vaughan, *The Commonweal,* May 9, 1941.)

Pope Leo's statement that the Church would "bring forth more abundant fruits if, in addition to liberty, she enjoyed the favor of the laws and the patronage of the public authority," is true enough as a general statement. But given the historical memory of religious strife, the development of the "lay" State, the well-beloved tradition of the United States, the temperament of its people, and the proud record of almost two centuries of religious liberty, it becomes very doubtful whether any Church in America that enjoyed the "favor of the laws" and the "patronage of public authority" would reap anything but a harvest of ill will, subversion from within, and unrelenting attack from without.

A spokesman for the same Leo, the outstanding theorist of Church-State relationship, once wrote: "It is the special property of human institutions and laws that there is nothing in them so holy and salutary but that custom may alter it, or time overthrow it, or social habits bring it to naught. So in the Church of God, in which changeableness of discipline is joined with absolute immutability of doctrine, it happens not rarely that things which were once apposite and suitable become in the course of time out of date, or useless or even harmful." (Letter, *Trans Oceanum,* 1896.)

Father John Courtney Murray, S.J., recently said of Leo: "His sense of the relativities of history was as fine as his sense of the absoluteness of doctrine." And it is that double sense that has determined Catholic polity through the ages.

Again, of the same Pope, Father Murray wrote: "He made

it clear that the Church-State relation is not an end in itself; it is importantly a matter of *vivendi disciplina*, which looks to the temporal and eternal welfare of man, who is both citizen and Christian." In the United States—even in the U.S. of that highly improbable future when non-Catholics have shriveled to a "numerically insignificant" portion of the population—the Christian is, and will be, an American, with an American's political beliefs, sentiments, and tradition. It is sometimes overlooked that if conversions to Catholicism became so strikingly numerous, American Catholics would be largely recent Protestants. A "Catholic" America would certainly differ in many respects from those nations whose traditions are rooted in the medieval period and for whom political and religious loyalties have long been so inextricably tangled that heresy is looked upon as treason.

This is not to say that if such a transformation were to come over America and we were to become a people of almost one religious mind there would be no changes. Every radical change in any country begets other changes; that is no more than an obvious law of history. And it is a law particularly consonant with democracy. If we all became Quakers, for instance, or most of us did, I presume that our foreign policy would shift from its present military emphasis. If we all became Adventists, or most of us did, I presume that Sunday would no longer be America's day of rest. If we all became Methodists, or most of us did, I presume there would be fewer bars on Third Avenue. And I presume also that if we all became Catholics, there would be revision of our divorce laws, there would be public recognition of certain holydays and a hundred and one other changes.

But it seems reasonable, and in keeping with the usual procedure of Catholicism, to conclude that these changes

would take place within the framework of the hallowed political institutions and traditions of America. A United States
turned Catholic would not necessarily be another Spain, any
more than Italy is Spain, or Ireland is Italy, or Bavaria is
France. Nor is there reason to believe that a goodly majority
of Catholics in any country means, inevitably, a "Catholic
State"—which, whatever its classroom vigor as a creature of
logic, has largely disappeared from the real world.*

The question voiced by Mr. Will Herberg in his contribution to this book is an insistent query heard wherever the
"Catholic problem" is discussed: "What are the long-range
purposes and intentions of the Church in these matters?" In
other words, is the Church working to foist a Spanish-style,
"un-American" pattern on America?

I sympathize with the questioners, but wonder if what some
of them are asking for is not so much a statement of intention as a repudiation of the theological doctrines that provide
the logical framework for the "Catholic State" thesis. If the
latter be it, Catholics will never be able to give them the
answer they want—and there are many, I know, who will not
be satisfied unless the Church renounces its claim of being
uniquely the Church of Christ. If, however, like Mr. Herberg,
they are asking for an official assurance that the textbook
spook from Ryan and Boland's *Catholic Principles of Politics*

---

* Father Murray, writing in the *American Ecclesiastical Review*, a
clerical journal, asks: "Did the Catholic 'thesis' go out with the Bourbons?
And do we now hover in midair, as it were, clutching our collective
principles to our collective bosom, unable to make any application of
them (save where there is dictatorship on the Bourbon model, as in
Spain), and condemned to find our way through the contemporary
world into the future (which belongs, I hope, to democracy) touching
only on the precarious footing of expediency, what time we look back
over our shoulder at the diminishing figure of Isabella II? What an extraordinary posture for the universal Church!"

is not likely to assume flesh and blood on American soil, such assurance has already been given by the most official spokesmen of American Catholicism.

In 1948, Archbishop John T. McNicholas, speaking for the American bishops as chairman of the Administrative Board of the National Catholic Welfare Conference, said: "We deny absolutely and without qualification that the Catholic Bishops of the United States are seeking a union of Church and State by any endeavors whatsoever, either proximately or remotely. If tomorrow Catholics constituted a majority in our country, they would not seek a union of Church and State. They would, then as now, uphold the Constitution and all its Amendments, recognizing the moral obligation imposed upon all Catholics to observe and defend the Constitution and its Amendments."

Two years earlier than this, Pope Pius XII wrote: "The increasingly frequent contacts between different religious professions, mingled indiscriminately in the same nation, have caused civil authorities to follow the principles of tolerance and liberty of conscience. In fact, there is a political tolerance, a civil tolerance, in regard to adherents of other religious beliefs which, in circumstances such as these, is a moral duty for Catholics." Again, in November, 1953, he told an audience of Italian Catholic jurists that "the duty to repress religious and moral deviation cannot . . . be an ultimate norm for action. It must be subordinated to higher and more general norms, which in some circumstances permit and even make it perhaps appear as the better part not to impede error in order to promote a greater good."

But *can* the American tradition of Church-State separation be reconciled with Catholic teaching? The answer is yes, provided one does not identify the American idea with an extreme and doctrinaire liberalism that would turn "democracy" into a full-blown ideology and root our political liberty in the proposition that skepticism is the only true religious philosophy for an American, indifferentism the only true religious attitude, relativism and subjectivism the only true outlook on morality.

For instance, it seems in some circles to be good "liberal" doctrine that "man is a law unto himself," or, in other words, that individual judgment and choice confer upon the one making them a moral "right" to do, or write, or say what he pleases. This, of course, is based on the notion that there is no objective wrong or right or, if there is, that the line where the moral law is drawn is too hazy for modern man.

Another popular belief has it that mere political authority (in this country the required number of votes) is the only real sanction a positive law needs. Thus, if tomorrow euthanasia were to become the law of the land, one need not consider it in relation to any natural or divine law; the political authority backing it up would be enough.

Both these ideas are completely out of harmony with Catholic thought. Indeed, they were specifically, and vigorously, condemned by Pope Leo XIII. If American democracy were actually founded on such principles—as apparently many people are beginning to think—then the critics of Catholicism would be right: Catholicism and Americanism would be wholly incompatible. The United States would be a monument to moral relativism and freewheeling secularism.

But is the American concept of civil liberties, or civil rights, rooted in such a philosophy? I think not. Our fathers in this country neither denied the objective moral law nor glorified the omnipotent state. They began the Declaration of Independence with the idea that there are such things as human rights that transcend whatever claims the State might make. Moreover, they defined these rights as God-given.

Then they went on with the understanding that the actions and functions of the State were necessarily controlled by recognition of these God-given rights. Their theory does not come under the heading of what Leo XIII condemned as "liberalism." When people equate the American doctrine with the beliefs the continental liberalists incarnated in the Third French Republic, they are, I think, doing violence to the American idea itself.

Much confusion arises from the dual use of the simple word "rights." A right may express a moral empowerment (as the right to marry, the right to a living wage), or it may express a negative moral immunity. The Bill of Rights, for instance, is actually a bill of prohibitions. When we speak of "civil rights," it is generally this sense that we have in mind. Religious liberty means that I am free from any State coercion where theological belief or worship is concerned. Free speech means that I need not fear a policeman every time I say something erroneous, stupid, irrational, controversial, unconventional, or unorthodox.

American civil rights are based on the idea that there are certain areas where the State calls a halt on its own powers—better, where the people themselves call a halt on the State. There are certain key aspects of life which Americans have simply put beyond the competence of the political authority.

Civil rights are *not* based on the idea that the citizen, by virtue of being an American, somehow gains a positive right, independent of the objective moral law or any other reality, to evolve his own morality. If I choose to accept this fashionable position, I remain free, of course, as far as the State goes, from any interference with my belief. But I have not, for that reason, been given any reason to stamp my philosophy with the Seal of the United States. No militia will move in if I hold that all religions are equally true (or equally false), for instance, but that doesn't necessarily objectify my belief or make it an American patriotic touchstone.

Our forefathers served us well. From a practical distrust of unnecessary State interference, they limited political authority drastically on such questions as religion, culture, and the exchange of ideas. Their concept of government succeeded in serving persons of many beliefs without destroying the claims of orthodoxy.

The important distinction they drew was one between society and the State (the political instrument of society). To certain voluntary social groupings (today, the churches, education, labor unions, employers' associations, fraternal organizations) they wisely reserved functions that can better— and with much less danger to liberty—be performed by free communities with no weapon but the doctrine of consent. The minimum needed to maintain public order and the basic requirements of the positive common good were the standards they chose to measure the empowerments given their brave new adventure in government.

These are still the standards by which Americans judge overt police action or State interference in the political, cultural, and religious areas of life. When such issues arise it is usually beside the point to belabor the errors of the "liberal" philosophy itself, or even the monstrous aberrations that often claim immunity from State interference, as Catholics often do, or to defend a wishy-washy indifferentism as *the* "American" philosophy, as the butcher-paper weeklies tend to do. Essentially it is not the idea put forth in the controversial movie, play, or book that civil liberty defends—nor even, in the strict sense, the author's moral "right to say it."

What is in question is whether the forced suppression is absolutely necessary if public order is to be maintained, whether the suppression is positively required by the demands of the common good. All Americans, it seems to me, should be very, very slow to call a cop in these cases. As a general rule, public order and the common good are best served by trusting, as our fathers did, in the free exchange of ideas. As long as we are free, the good, the true, and the beautiful will usually get a sympathetic hearing.

Antipathy to Catholicism is not merely based on suspicion of Catholic theories and writings on Church and State. We cannot, I think, lose sight of the fact that as Catholics we do not conform to many now-popular beliefs about religion and morality (divorce and birth control, for example—and perhaps soon, euthanasia). Much of the criticism hurled against the Church in political terms is really a protest, psychological in origin, against Catholic theology. In a country where approximately one out of every three marriages ends in the divorce courts, there is bound to be strong resentment against the Church that solemnly brands subsequent matings as adulterous. A Church that proclaims from the housetops that contraception is always against the law of God will naturally arouse the fierce antagonism of those who practice contraception and deem themselves virtuous when they do.

As American culture becomes more secularized and further cut off from its Christian roots, we can expect this kind of antagonism to increase. We can expect, too, that protests against Catholic theology will continue to be framed in political rather than in theological terms, if only because theology has become largely meaningless to so many of those who resent the Church's insistence on an unchanging moral order and abiding Natural Law.

In days gone by, Catholic doctrine was condemned as being un-Biblical or superstitious: the judgment was theological. Today, it is more often branded as "undemocratic" or "un-American." This, it seems to me, is a telltale sign of the growing totalitarianization of "democracy." American democracy is traditionally a tolerant political way of life. Many would now like to make of it a set of secularist dogmas by which all things, even the moral order and religious beliefs, are measured. The professional birth-controllers, the divorce-apologists (perhaps soon, the euthanasiasts), and the aggressive secularists generally more and more have taken to wrapping their beliefs in the Stars and Stripes. They are increasingly ready to put all who disagree with them outside the "democratic" pale.

We cannot lose sight of the fact, either, that as Catholics we frankly subscribe to an ecclesiasticism that is nondemocratic. For many, that is reason enough to doubt the sincerity of our belief in political democracy. Especially for those who regard democracy not merely as a technique of government and a political philosophy but as a kind of substitute for religion, our acceptance of an *authoritarian* Church (which is not at all the same as *totalitarian* Church—actually a meaningless phrase) is anomalous.

In the Catholic scheme spiritual authority is all-important and the popular will has little or no effect on the government of the Church. If it were proved beyond doubt, for instance, that most American Catholics thought birth prevention was a good idea, the Church would still hold fast to its teaching that contraception is against the law of God. The Church is democratic only in the sense that the son of a chimney sweep may sit on the papal throne or a bricklayer's boy may wear the scarlet robes of a cardinal.

To the Catholic, the Church's authoritarian spirit and hierarchical structure are logical and even desirable. (This is, of course, not to condone abuses and exaggerations of clerical authority.) Neither our ecclesiology nor our theology is Protestant, and a great deal of confusion could be avoided if that were kept clearly in mind. Both Protestants and Catholics, in this country where theological understanding is dim, often make the mistake of discounting each other's basic beliefs, so that Protestants are judged as if they were indecisive Catholics and Catholics as if they were bamboozled Protestants.

Given the concept of the priesthood, which is essential in Catholicism, hierarchy is inevitable. Given the charge to "go, teach all nations," how can one expect the Church to be other than authoritarian? Given the belief that the Church is preserved by God from teaching religious error, how can one expect it to determine doctrine by testing popular opinion? How, logically, can the Church shift its moral pronouncements to fit the winds of the popular will? It is of the nature of the Church to be unyielding and absolutist where faith and morals are concerned, because—Catholics believe—the truth which the Church is divinely empowered to teach is unchanging and the morality it upholds is based on the immutable law of God.

All this a Catholic believes. If he did not, he would not be a Catholic. The question is, are such beliefs incompatible with American democracy?

The question is pointed up by the fact that some of the Church's basic moral teachings have direct consequence on the political behavior of Catholics. The doctrinal position on birth control, for instance, does not exist in a political vacuum.

In two states, Massachusetts and Connecticut, Catholics acting as citizens have been called upon to decide whether certain ancient anticontraceptive laws should be removed from
the statute books. This is generally held to be one of the key
issues in the Catholics-and-democracy question. Whenever the
subject is discussed, there is sure to be some mention of it.

Catholics as Americans are certainly free to believe what
they choose about the morality of birth control, the argument
goes, but they have no right to inflict the Church's teachings
on those who believe otherwise.

The plain fact, of course, is that there has been no general
attempt on the part of Catholics to put anti-birth-control laws
on the books of any state. The laws in Massachusetts and
Connecticut were drafted by legislators, mostly Protestants,
at a time when Catholics were not alone in holding that contraception was a morally heinous practice. Catholics, as
voters and legislators in these states, are being asked, not
whether the state should begin to legislate against contraception, but whether the present laws should be maintained.
(This is something else again than "imposing" a law.)

What should the Catholic citizen, as a good democrat, do
in a case like that? Should he refrain from voting so that in
places where he is in the majority, decision will be made by
the minority? Or should he vote against his conscience? To
ask either of him, it seems to me, is something less than
democratic.

Perhaps it may be held that he should not let his conscience
be formed by the moral teachings of the Catholic Church.
But that hardly seems in keeping with our tradition that *how*
an American forms his conscience—whether according to the
principles of a rationalist philosophy, his private interpreta-

tion of the Bible, or the moral theology of the Catholic Church—is of no political significance.

It seems to me that the test of one's belief in democracy is in how well one accepts the will of the majority. The spirit in which Catholics accept the overriding of a law in which they believe is the real test, not the zeal with which they use their democratic rights to maintain a law already on the books.

Admittedly, a Catholic cannot in conscience vote for birth prevention, but he is under no obligation to multiply laws. There are many states in the union that do not have anti-contraceptive laws, and as far as I know there is no move on the part of Catholics to introduce any.

Oddly enough, some of the most bitter critics of Catholicism in America are found in the group that once succeeded in making its own belief about the evil of alcohol into a Constitutional Amendment and is constantly active in promoting antigambling legislation, sometimes with clear success.

I know of no comparable examples of Catholics actively engaged in trying to make their singular moral beliefs into law. But as American culture moves further away from traditional Christian morality, there will certainly be recurrent efforts on the part of Catholics to uphold existing legislation. I do not think the present assault on traditional Christian morality will stop at birth prevention; it will go on to hasten the tomb with the same energy with which it emptied the womb. Not too many years hence there may be widespread attempts to blot out the present legislation against euthanasia. And that prospect sums up the real problem of Catholics and American democracy. If the time comes when concerted efforts are made to legalize mercy killing, Catholics are sure to use their privileges to maintain the present prohibitions against it. To ask us to act otherwise, it seems to me, is to require that we abandon our moral (and, one might add, democratic) responsibility for the society in which we live.

On such questions the position of the Church is final and absolute: birth prevention and mercy killing are everlastingly wrong and the Church will ever hold to that position. Catholics, because they believe as they do, will never put their approval on these practices and will positively work against them. As far as basic morality goes, we are shameless absolutists.

The democratic state, on the other hand, in Reinhold Niebuhr's words, is "at least provisionally relativist in not permitting any definition of the truth to infringe upon 'the rule of the majority.'" But, in the words which William P. Clancy used in introducing this series, "the tyranny of a majority that rejects all absolute morality is a refinement in horror which it has taken the modern world to discover. It is this horror which the democratic absolutists seem to offer in the name of enlightenment, and it is against this threat that religious men react."

Taking both these statements as true then, it seems to me that the real challenge facing Catholics is how to undergird American democracy with the principles of unchanging morality for which the Church is today almost the sole remaining consistent spokesman. Jacques Maritain has written: "Not only does the democratic state of mind proceed from the inspiration of the Gospel, but it cannot exist without it." And in an allocution to the Roman Rota on October 2, 1945, Pope Pius XII had this to say of democracy: "A democracy in which there is no common agreement at least as to the fundamental maxims of life, especially as to the rights of God, the dignity of the human person, respect for honest work and personal freedom, even politically such a democracy would be defective and precarious. Therefore, when the people abandon the Christian faith, or fail to maintain it firmly as the principle of civil life, democracy easily becomes corrupt and is apt to degenerate eventually into a party totalitarianism or authoritarianism."

Clearly, there is a great need for Catholic participation in political life. But that participation has to be scrupulously based on democracy's own terms. It will not do, for instance, to call a friendly cop arbitrarily to close down a movie house showing an unacceptable film. Highhandedness of that kind only outrages Americans who jealously value their political freedom. In the long run it weakens the influence of the Church as a persuading force. It is widely, and bitterly, interpreted as nothing better than contempt for the accepted processes of democracy. It actually plays straight into the hands of the latter-day apostles of "democratic" totalitarianism. These men, posing as the true voice of American democracy, are delighted when doubt is cast on those who do not share their own grandiose ideas of what is and is not "democratic." Nothing suits their designs better than for the impression to be abroad that Catholics, who above all others challenge their secularism, actually hold democracy in contempt.

I think also that we make a serious mistake when we insist on trivial external acknowledgments of religion in public life as if somehow such symbols, no matter how grudgingly given, canceled out the true fact that America is increasingly secularist. Mere formal prayer in public-school classrooms or on state occasions, for instance, may mean nothing more than an empty gesture, and the aggressiveness necessary to instate such a

formality, sometimes against vigorous objection, often con-
fuses the issue as to just what Catholics are up to.

I know there are zealous Catholic groups who feel it is a
great triumph for Christianity when they succeed in convincing a merchant that it would be smart business practice were
he to feature a crèche in his show window during the Christmas season, or who otherwise use the threat of withholding
money or votes to buy "religious" gestures. But I think they
are greatly underestimating the real task of Christians in the
modern world and confuse symbols with realities. A show-
window Christianity offers no hope of salvation.

The religious mind, it seems, is particularly tempted to indulge in self-righteous posturings—to stand aside heaping
anathemas on the false philosophies guiding the world and
predicting doomsday, while the world, heedless, goes on
about its business. There is surely a comforting satisfaction
in regularly reassuring ourselves that we are right while the
heathen are wrong, and in pointing out, generally in pat formulas, all the errors into which fellow Americans are slipping.
But what good does it do for us to talk only to ourselves? Of
what use is it merely to decry the fact that the Name of God
is not acknowledged at the UN, for instance, if we do not
make the Name of God meaningful for those who guide the
UN? How persuasive is the illiberal castigation of a false liberalism? How convincing is the undemocratic defense of true
democracy? Or the philistine-tempered denunciation of a misguided intellectualism? They give the impression that Catholics despise values which in reality the Church cherishes.

Maritain, in his little book on *Christianity and Democracy,*
has summed up the challenge facing American Catholics: "The
important thing for the political life of the world and for the
solution of this crisis of civilization is by no means to pretend

that Christianity is linked to democracy and that the Christian faith compels every believer to be a democrat; it is to affirm that democracy is linked to Christianity and that the democratic impulse has arisen in human history as a temporal manifestation of the inspiration of the Gospel. The question does not deal here with Christianity as a religious creed and road to eternal life, but rather with Christianity as leaven in the social and political life of nations and as bearer of the temporal hope of mankind."

The challenge is one of meaningful participation in, not sullen withdrawal from, American democratic life. If Catholic participation in democracy is to be effective in producing the leaven of Christianity in America's political life, it must be *democratic* participation: the participation of Catholics, acting as citizens, who are infinitely respectful of democratic institutions and ever alert to defend the civil rights of all Americans. The terms of such participation are that it seek no special privileges for the Church and wait with the patience of the Lord for the acceptance of grace. What we sometimes forget is that though we cheerfully accept the authority of the Church, believing as we do, others without our faith do not. We cannot rely on the appeal of authority to do our work for us in the temporal order.

Daniel F. Cleary

CATHOLICS
AND POLITICS

C ATHOLICS are in politics as they are in all phases of American life. But Catholics are not engaged in politics as Catholics. Politically speaking, to be a Catholic in the United States usually means merely to be an American who happens to be a Catholic. This is as it should be. As voters, however, American Catholics have had a considerable impact on their nation's political life.

Catholics should vote as their conscience dictates, with the needs of the times and the common good kept in mind. They do not always do so. Neither do the rest of Americans. Conscientious voting presumes a study of the issues and an intelligent appraisal of the candidates in a campaign. That takes more effort than many voters are willing to make, since it is not easy to understand our foreign and domestic problems.

Properly distributed, less than three million votes, no matter whose, would have been enough to elect Adlai E. Stevenson in 1952 or Thomas E. Dewey in 1948. Some three million Catholic voters, out of the total Catholic vote, heavily concentrated where the electoral votes are also concentrated, had a lot to do with putting General Eisenhower in the White House. They had just as much to do (maybe more) with putting Harry S. Truman back in office in 1948. This writer believes these Catholic voters made the switch for the same reasons that their non-Catholic compatriots made it. Leaving aside the objective question as to whether the change was actually for the nation's benefit or not, I think the switch was made because those voters felt that their own individual economic interest would benefit and because of an emotional response to largely irrelevant appeals to their prejudices.

Until recently, Catholics could be counted on to vote consistently in the same way from city to city, year in and year out. During the last hundred years American Catholics have tended to be concentrated in the big cities—chiefly in the industrial East and Middle West. It was during this period that they established themselves as the predominant element in the local Democratic political organizations (which made a strong bid for the immigrant vote) as well as in labor unions. Because of ethnic origins Catholics were found largely in the lower and lower-middle economic groups.

Before 1932 these Catholics looked to the local Democratic political organizations for jobs, Christmas baskets, and relief in the big cities. And as the Catholic population grew in numbers and political influence, Catholics began to take over control of local party machinery in many urban areas. Because of their numbers in organizable occupations they were also rising in prominence in the American labor movement.

But with the advent of the New Deal social program these workers and their families tended more and more to look to Washington rather than to the local party chieftain for aid. And a reasonable expectation of future favors, which is the basis for gratitude in political life, kept a large body of Catholics solidly behind the Democrats on the national level between 1932 and 1944. Moreover, Franklin D. Roosevelt proved to be so superb a vote-getter—he was clearly the best precinct captain in every city organization—that the local chiefs permitted their organizations to go to seed. F.D.R. got the vote out for them. Hence the local politicos got out of condition and failed to see what was happening to their once-effective machines.

Meanwhile the breadlines were getting rarer, and the number of Catholics who needed help from the government was growing smaller. Before 1930 the rare Catholic who moved to the suburbs, after climbing out of the lower-middle income group, frequently became first a Mason and then a Republican. For years Catholics at country clubs were even rarer than Democrats. But by 1950 it was possible to "belong" and still be a Catholic, though hardly a Catholic and a Democrat as well. So the children of people who had looked to the ward leader for their jobs went off to the suburbs and joined the station-wagon set, wearing their brand-new Republicanism as a badge of responsibility. They were so secure now that they saw no possible need of future favors from any hard-hatted political boss. Their problems were different, too. They were beginning to suffer the pangs of income taxes every March 15. The sons of the men who during the Depression had tried to get lined up with WPA were chafing under the price controls of OPA. If they knew the story about the man once saved from death that ends, "Well, what have you done for me lately?" they never applied it to themselves.

By election time of 1952, the move to the suburbs had reached tremendous proportions. In one metropolitan area after another, the population of the peripheral districts came to exceed that of the city itself. Department stores in New York, Chicago, Washington, and other cities acknowledged this phenomenon by following their customers to the suburbs.

It was not altogether surprising that in these prosperous outlying areas Ike buttons were thicker in the fall of 1952 than carbon monoxide.

In all, the Catholics who vote probably number only twelve million out of the sixty million who went to the polls in November, 1952. Some of these voted Republican in 1952 because they had changed their social status to a very large extent. It is true that a large segment of second- and third-generation Irish, Germans, Poles, and Italians, who make up the bulk of the urban Catholic vote, stayed with the Democrats right to the end. But their children, who became old enough to vote in 1946 and thereafter, had never learned at firsthand what a depression is; as a result they did not have the same motivation, or memories, behind their votes as the people who lived through the 1921-1932 period and started voting about 1928. As voters, Catholics and non-Catholics alike tend to take on the political coloration of the economic class in which they either find themselves or to which they are currently aspiring. If the Eisenhower Administration kicks the suburbanites around economically, they will, I am sure, "turn the rascals out" at the first opportunity.

In a land where the secret ballot prevails, it is difficult to determine how Catholics vote, except in those few areas where they constitute the predominant majority of the electorate. It is considerably easier to evaluate the impact of Catholic office-holders on their nation's political life, particularly as the present emphasis on publicizing every facet of a candidate's personal life includes making his religion almost as well known as his political party.

The number of Catholics who appeared on television screens during the Kefauver crime investigation was embarrassing to their coreligionists around the country. They were not labeled as Catholics, of course, when their faces or hands were televised, but the follow-up stories in the newspapers frequently found occasion to bring out the church affiliations of the reluctant witnesses and derelict public officials who squirmed under Rudolph Halley's questioning.

I do not think this pinpointing of the defection of Catholics in public office is evidence of any "Protestant plot." I believe that people expect Catholics in public office to know better, and to adhere to a stricter moral code, than colleagues who do not have the benefit of very specific religious principles to guide them. It is therefore a greater cause for scandal when a politician caught with his hand in the till turns out to be a Catholic.

The same must be said of the unscrupulous Catholic businessman, professional man, labor leader, or just plain citizen. To be a Catholic in America, as elsewhere, carries with it the responsibility to live in such a way as to bring nothing but credit on the Church. There are undoubtedly some Catholic politicians who parade their membership in the Church and make political capital out of it but whose political conduct leaves much to be desired. But there are, happily, many examples of Catholics in elective public office who are a credit to their Church.

It should be noted that there is currently no Catholic on the United States Supreme Court. Just as there is, traditionally at least, one Catholic in the Cabinet, so there has usually been one Catholic on the Court. Since Frank Murphy's death that has not been true. The President is under no obligation to appoint a Catholic to any position, but in recognition of the fact that Catholics constitute about one-fifth of the total population, it has been deemed equitable and perhaps politically expedient to allocate a certain number of top appointive positions to members of the Roman Catholic Church. In the cities and in state governments, the Catholics are in government positions pretty much in the same ratio as that of the Catholic population to the total population in the city or state.

Catholics in office do not act *as* Catholics, in any sectarian sense, and they should not. That is to say, they should not be forever looking out for the temporal interests of the Church. They are not agents of the Church, nor are they representatives (or even necessarily representative) of their coreligionists. But they *should* conduct themselves as good Catholics, in or out of office. The best interests of the entire country determine what the position of the individual Catholic legislator or administrator should be.

There can be, and indeed are, instances where an individual Catholic lawmaker or administrator must in conscience vote or administer contrary to the expressed wishes of the Catholic hierarchy and large segments of the laity. This is due to the fact (too little known to non-Catholics) that one Catholic will not necessarily agree with any other Catholic on purely temporal matters, even though the other Catholic happens to be his bishop. There is no "Catholic" position on tidelands oil, for instance, or on public power.

Of course, in areas of dogma where the Church, as differentiated from individual churchmen, has spoken, the Catholic is bound in conscience to act in accordance with the moral law, as expounded by the Church. But this obligation to follow conscience is no less binding upon non-Catholics, although they may elect, as long as they are outside the Church, to disagree on specific moral issues.

What people call the "Catholic vote" cannot be "delivered" to any candidate or party. Nor, for that matter, can the labor vote, the Jewish vote, or the Lutheran vote. Catholics are by no means a politically monolithic group. To be accurate, one should really refer to Catholics who vote, as distinguished from the "Catholic vote," which is a nonexistent commodity.

Despite occasional deviation (especially in recent years) by individuals, the hierarchy and lower clergy of the Church realize that political questions are rarely such as to justify electioneering on their part. It may well be that in future years it will be the normal thing for most Catholics to be Republicans, even as in former years they tended for tribal and economic reasons to vote Democratic. Certainly, it is no part of Catholic dogma that they should vote one way or the other, even though the Baltimore Catechism does spell out the responsibility of all Catholics to vote for the best man and always in the public interest.

The worthiness of politics as a Christian vocation should be hammered home to the young, many of whom will inevitably gravitate to politics as their career. They should be prepared to recognize that since politics is a Christian vocation, they are bound to conduct themselves in a way not to conflict with Christian principles. Catholic colleges have not paid enough attention to political science or public administration as possible careers for their graduates. If we expect the graduates to participate intelligently in public affairs, perhaps the addition of sound courses in these areas is needed in the curriculums of our Catholic colleges and universities.

But there is no need for pessimism on the subject of Catholics in American politics. Our officeholders, perhaps, need to be reminded that much is expected of them because they are Catholics, and that they will have to render an ultimate accounting. We all need to be reminded that party labels are of little significance in doing the right thing in politics. We need to be reminded that secularism is no better in the sight of God than Communism, and that we stand in much greater danger of embracing secularism. We need to be reminded that we have a positive duty to work for improvement of the temporal order largely through the existing political machinery.

Under no circumstances should a "ghetto" mentality develop among Catholics with regard to politics in America. The Catholic War Veterans are probably the epitome of this kind of attitude. If there are problems that warrant the attention and existence of a group of war veterans, why divide the veterans among the various sects?

So also with politics. I do not believe there is room or even need for a Catholic political party in America. There is definitely a need for Catholics to participate knowledgeably and industriously in all aspects of the political scene, national, state, and local, as voters, legislators, administrators, and judges.

James O'Gara

THE CATHOLIC
ISOLATIONIST

A POUND and a half of lard, two pounds of flour, four small cans of condensed milk, and a two-pound bag of dried beans or peas—these are the items that went into the Eisenhower food parcel. To get their hands on one, in the summer of 1953, East Germans streamed across the border into the West by the thousands, thumbing their noses at their Communist masters, daring the Russian tanks to intervene, risking prison and even death.

While this mass disobedience was embarrassing East German officials, U.S. leaders were facing a different kind of problem. All over the nation, farm surpluses piled higher and higher. Wheat spilled over its bins, the barns were filled to the bursting point. From three to five billion dollars' worth of farm surplus was already on hand, and the fall harvest was not yet in. For U.S. government officials, the problem involves more than the embarrassment of being almost shamefully rich in a world of poverty; on a purely physical plane, there is simply not enough storage space to accommodate the surplus riches of the U.S. agricultural system.

The chasm between East German want and U.S. wealth is typical of the modern era. The same stark contrast of poverty on one hand and plenty on the other exists between the U.S. and India, Italy, China, and a large part of the rest of the world. Back of the U.S. surplus stands the vast productive power of this nation, the natural resources, the technological development, what is called the know-how, for the ability to produce farm surpluses is essentially the same as that which spews out automobiles and trucks, tanks and planes, devices and gadgets of all sorts in an ever-expanding stream. What all this wealth and productive potential adds up to is national power, on a scale never dreamed of by the Founding Fathers.

Young as nations go, the United States now exercises power on a scale so vast that an important decision in Washington affects the lives of individuals living thousands of miles away, in Pakistan and Korea, in Paris and Berlin, in the Moscow of Malenkov and Molotov as well as the Moscow located in Idaho. Whether the average U.S. citizen is ready to recognize it or not, and whether he likes it or not, American power is a fact, one of the most important facts in the modern world. Because of this power, the future of the world for many years to come hinges to a large extent on the answer to this question: In foreign affairs, will the United States match its awesome power with a corresponding sense of responsibility? If the U.S. uses its power justly and intelligently, peace is possible. If the U.S. abdicates its responsibility, peace in our time is an impossibility.

As far as American Catholics are concerned, one would expect the weight of opinion to be on the side of an intelligent recognition of U.S. power in world affairs and a responsible exercise of that power. In matters of foreign policy, one would expect American Catholics to have before their eyes the goal of an international order in conformity with the Christian principles of justice and charity. Inclining Catholics in this direction is the universality of the Church, which knows neither race nor nationality but is intended for all men, in every age and in every land, and which sees all men as brothers under the Fatherhood of God. In the Mystical Body all are joined with Christ; Englishmen, Frenchmen, Americans, Russians, Germans, Chinese, Japanese, white, black, yellow, and red— all are made one.

By definition, by what they profess, whatever their individual day-to-day failings, Catholics subscribe to the law of love. It cannot be a matter of indifference that millions in other parts of the world regularly fail to get enough to eat, or that in countries like India and Egypt the average baby has less than an even chance of surviving until he is twenty-five. Although applying the parable of the Good Samaritan to the affairs of nations is not as simple as it is in the case of individuals, and the forms it takes will be different, it must still be applied.

The whole weight of Catholic social thought inclines toward solidarity, in families, in industrial relations, in the international order. It is opposed to division, *laissez faire,* anarchy. In making statements on international affairs, the modern popes have merely applied this idea to our times. It is not surprising, therefore, that they have spoken against a spirit of national isolationism and selfishness in world affairs. The teaching authority of the modern papacy has been strongly exercised on behalf of the organization of nations, the creation of an international juridical order, and collective action against unjust aggressors. At the same time the popes have emphasized the necessity of achieving social justice if real peace is to be created, and they have stressed such points as the need to permit have-not nations access to raw materials and markets and to allow citizens of overpopulated countries entry into less crowded areas of the world. Quotations to document the internationalist position of the modern papacy could be endless; a few typical ones will suffice.

In 1928, Pope Pius XI wrote in his encyclical, *Mortalium Animos:*

On this side and on that, longstanding discords and new differences provoke seditions and internal struggles, and many controversies which jeopardize the tranquillity and prosperity of peoples can never be solved save by the joint actions of heads of States or those who direct or administer the country's interests. And so it is very easy to understand the longings of a great many people to see, in the name of this universal brotherhood, the establishment of an even closer and closer union between the various nations, all the more because all acknowledge the unity of the human race.

In his Christmas Message of 1948, Pope Pius XII wrote:

The Catholic doctrine on the State and civil society has always been based on the principle that, in keeping with the will of God, the nations form together a community with a common aim and common duties. Even when the proclamation of this principle and its practical consequences gave rise to violent reactions, the Church denied her assent to the erroneous concept of an absolutely autonomous sovereignty divested of all social obligations.

After World War I, Pope Benedict XV wrote in his encyclical, *Pacem Dei Munus:*

. . . it is much to be desired, Venerable Brethren, that all States, putting aside mutual suspicion, should unite in one league, or rather a type of family of peoples, calculated both to maintain their own independence and safeguard the order of human society.

Speaking to the fourth annual Congress of the World Movement for Federal Government in April of 1951, Pope Pius XII said:

The Catholic Isolationist

Your movement, gentlemen, dedicates itself to realizing an effective political organization of the world. Nothing is more in conformity with the traditional doctrine of the Church. . . .

On the subject of aggression, Pope Pius XII wrote in his Christmas Message of 1948:

A people threatened with an unjust aggression, or already its victim, may not remain passively indifferent if it would act and think as becomes Christians; all the more does the solidarity of the family of nations forbid others to behave as mere spectators in an attitude of apathetic neutrality. Who will ever measure the harm already caused in the past by such indifference to war of aggression, which is quite alien to the Christian instinct? One thing however is certain: the commandment of peace is a matter of divine law. Its purpose is the protection of the goods of humanity, inasmuch as they are the gifts of the Creator. Among these goods some are of such importance to society that it is perfectly lawful to defend them against unjust aggression. *Their defense is even an obligation for the nations as a whole who have a duty not to abandon a nation that is attacked.* [Italics added.]

On the subject of the United Nations, Pope Pius XII wrote in his 1944 Christmas Message:

This organization will be vested by common consent with supreme authority and with power to smother in its germinal stages any threat of isolated or collective aggression. No one can hail this development with greater joy than he who has long upheld the principle that the idea of war as an apt and appropriate means of solving international conflicts is now out of date. . . . If there is now the threat that other nations will intervene judicially and inflict chastisement on aggressors, then war will always be subject to the stigma of proscription, will be under surveillance, and will be open to prevention by force. Thus, mankind, emerging from the dark night in which it has been so long submerged, will be able to hail the dawn of a new and better era of history.

So say the popes. But only non-Catholics will be surprised that many U.S. Catholics act as if they have never heard of such papal statements, or, if they have heard them, still ignore them. American Catholics traditionally have a very high regard for the person of the pope, whoever he may be. European Catholics even have a somewhat cynical remark to the effect that when the pope sneezes, U.S. Catholics wipe their noses. But the pope pronouncing on the Assumption and the pope making a specific application of Catholic principle to the social order or the international scene are two different things. For many American Catholics there appear to be more intellectual, moral, and emotional roadblocks in the way of accepting papal social thought than there are preventing unquestioning assent to an infallible papal pronouncement on a matter of strict dogma.

Perhaps if one could take the long view, this lag between what the popes preach on international affairs and American Catholic practice would not seem a matter for too great concern. It took a long time for the papal social encyclicals like *Rerum Novarum* and *Quadragesimo Anno* even to begin to enter into popular currency, but that process is now well started, and in late years the social encyclicals have almost imperceptibly come to be respectable. If one could hope for as much in attitudes on international affairs, the situation would look brighter than it actually does. But here the future is not too promising, and time is short. Like millions of other Americans, many Catholics in the U.S. draw the line at the water line. For them the Pacific and the Atlantic Oceans represent the ultimate range of interest and concern. As far as they are concerned, the rest of the world can go its way. Sink or swim, it apparently makes little difference to them.

In 1954, this attitude represents more than moral abdication in international affairs. It represents national suicide. The most pressing argument for what is called internationalism, as opposed to isolationism, is national self-interest. The days when the U.S. could debate on the League of Nations and reject the idea of participation without feeling any immediate effect are gone. Wendell Willkie's "One World" phrase was more than rhetoric. Modern science has devoured distance and made neighbors of us all. The birth of the atom bomb marked the beginning of a new era; isolationism is now a sheer impossibility for a nation of any size or importance. One way or the other, the hydrogen bomb will make men brothers; we will unite in life, or we will die together. There is no other way.

Isolationism in this country will decline in influence only when educators and the molders of public opinion have persuaded enough people that U.S. self-interest demands an intelligent participation in international affairs and prudent use of national power on behalf of international order and a world at peace. Here, then, there would seem to be all the ingredients for a happy marriage. On the one hand there is the national interest, and on the other Catholic predisposition toward creating a family of nations.

Yet, despite the many papal statements on the subject, important segments of Catholic opinion echo the worst tags of the isolationist-nationalistic press. Thus some diocesan papers and powerful columnists dutifully print current papal statements on the necessity for international organization, then editorially snipe at U.S. participation in the UN. Forced to the wall, such editors and columnists would agree that papal teaching is certainly on the side of an international world organization dedicated to keeping the peace. But not the UN, they will hasten to add, not the UN. The theory they will support, if pushed into a dialectical corner; the practice, the never-perfect reality, will not satisfy, today or ever.

For all the stress placed on logic by Catholic schools, the position of such Catholic isolationists would be less dangerous if it were not so illogical. A clear-cut withdrawal to our own shores by the U.S. would create a power vacuum into which the Soviet Union would move immediately. This would mean incalculable harm to the world, but even so this course would hardly be as dangerous to the national interest as the on-again, off-again position to which Catholic isolationists seem to be particularly susceptible. Cursed with a potentially fatal ambivalence, they will one day parrot the outcries of every shrill nationalist, alienating our allies, urging withdrawal from foreign entanglements, a halt to the "slaughter" of "our boys," an end to "global boondoggling," and lower taxes; the next day they are just as likely to fall easy prey to the most impassioned, carry-the-war-to-the-Communist-enemy orators. For this group, General MacArthur was made to order, and the same people who thought we should pull out of Korea were simultaneously almost hysterical in their support of the man who would have enlarged the war by carrying it to China proper.

Here the problem with the Catholic isolationist is not that he ignores the necessity of "pure means." Rather it is that he seems completely uninterested in the means by which decisions can be implemented, paying no attention to the fact that grand-sounding decisions in foreign affairs are useless, and even worse than useless, if no means exist to carry them out. As a result of this sublime indifference to the practical execution of policy, the Catholic isolationist lives in a kind of Walter Mitty world that has very little resemblance to the actual distribution of power among nations.

In consistently ignoring the limits of the possible in this way, the Catholic isolationist resembles many of his non-religious cohorts. But the Catholic isolationist has a special characteristic, apparently due to a never-stated assumption that moral judgments by individuals carry with them the persuading force of armies. Not for him the mundane assembling of divisions, the counting of planes, the massing of tanks. Once moral judgment is pronounced, the problem is solved. Thus rhetorical denunciations of the Chinese Communist regime are plentiful; down-to-earth estimates of the fighting force necessary to invade the mainland of China are few and far between. Questioning U.S. ability to launch such an attack at this time or the prudence of the entire idea at any time is likely to produce only the charge of being "soft" toward Communism.

Oddly enough, an important element in Catholic isolationism is distrust of foreigners. The child of an immigrant Church and himself frequently the son or daughter of immigrant parents, the Catholic isolationist is firmly, almost fanatically, nationalistic. In its broad outlines, this distaste for foreigners may be a quality which Catholic isolationists share with other Americans who have the same outlook on foreign policy. But Catholic isolationists excel in antipathy for people snidely referred to as "planners." As has been frequently noted, the roots of this fear go far back. In the last century, when Darwinism, scientism, anticlericalism, and modernism in general made the future of the Church look dark, Catholics withdrew so thoroughly from intellectual, social, and artistic movements that leadership fell largely to a-religious or actually antireligious men. As a result too many good features of the modern world developed without the influence of Catholics or even despite the spirited opposition of Catholics.

In this century, the same fear makes many American Catholics automatically unsympathetic to organizations like UNESCO, which grew up under non-Catholic auspices, and positively antagonistic to enthusiasts for world government or to those who dedicate their lives to planning organized ways and means of attacking world poverty. Both the late Brien McMahon, who was a Catholic, and Walter Reuther, who is not, separately proposed using daringly large sums—which were still much smaller than the amount spent on national defense—for years to come, in an effort to build up the poverty-stricken areas of the world and create a climate favorable to peace. It would be pleasant to be able to report that Catholic opinion made these suggestions its own, but outside of a limited circle it would be untrue. Among Catholic isolationists such schemes arouse profound mistrust, and this fact leads to one of the greatest paradoxes of Catholic isolationism: Although feeding the hungry and clothing the naked are works of mercy, some Catholic commentators do not merely disagree with but refer sneeringly to what they call the "do-gooders" and "bleeding hearts" active in Point Four or international organizations like UNESCO.

Part of the emotional underpinning of Catholic isolationism undoubtedly comes from the long-standing love affair between the American Catholic press and the simple solution. Until comparatively recent times, few statements could flout reality too baldly or contradict observable facts too obviously for solemn editorial approval, if only they sounded sufficiently moral. Any increase in the crime rate, for example, was obviously the result of the decline of religion; any attempt to discuss other, and perhaps more pertinent or proximate factors, was considered unnecessary. The social encyclicals stressed the need for a reform of social institutions as well as of individuals. Yet over the years many Catholic papers have been satisfied with echoing the pious platitude that people worry too much about reforming society when everyone knows that all our problems would be solved if only people would be better.

Added to this love for the oversimplified solution is a strong tendency, in Catholic groups and publications, to personify ideas or movements of which they disapprove on moral grounds. Thus Margaret Sanger often becomes not someone whose motives are known only to God but whose social theories on artificial birth prevention must be condemned, but a scheming woman who deliberately set out to disrupt the family, lead young people into sin, and ultimately destroy the American way of life. In the same way, many Catholics identified Stalin with Communism, and the triumph of Communism in China with Mao Tse-tung—or, more likely, with Dean Acheson and General George C. Marshall.

In the area of foreign affairs, this habit of personifying movements or forces is dangerous in the extreme, because it is easy to get the idea that all our problems would be solved if only Stalin were dead, or Malenkov, or Mao Tse-tung, or Beria, or Hirohito, or someone else. This is rarely the case, since the conduct of foreign affairs is at the best of times a complicated and tortuous business, and today is doubly so. But personifying evil has the advantage of keeping the problem small and—on the surface at least—within manageable proportions.

Nowhere does the predisposition to the simplistic show up more strikingly than on the question of Communism. For many American Catholics, Communism has long been the magic touchstone. If the Communists are for something, these Catholics are automatically against it. Despite the social teachings of the Church, and the labor of many devoted Catholics, clerical and lay, there is not much doubt that in many Catholic groups opposition to labor unions, public housing, slum clearance, efforts to win interracial justice and the like, is due to this absurd use of Communism as a negative determinant of what Catholics favor. In such circles the suggestion that Catholics might be for certain things which Communists also favor will produce nothing but suspicion and ostracism.

It should also be noted that the use of Communism as a magic yardstick works both ways; anyone vociferously "anti-Communist" is sacrosanct. Senator McCarran is a good example of this. The immigration policies he pushes through seem hardly in the spirit of the papal approach to world population problems. But he is very anti-Communist and "security-minded." Thus the nation was recently surprised by a well-known Jesuit's attacking in most heated terms the Jesuit weekly *America*, which had criticized Senator McCarran's immigration legislation; the Jesuit defended Senator McCarran's policies, apparently, because the Senator is anti-Communist, whatever Catholic population experts may think of his stand on immigration.

In discussing isolationism among American Catholics, the question of Communism is of key importance. Despite the many years in which the Catholic press has hammered away at Communism, it has almost always been in negative terms. Serious attempts to understand and explain Communism have been rare, and few Catholic publications have tried to give their readers an understanding of the dynamism and appeal of Communism. The many cartoonists who depicted Stalin with two locks of hair suggesting horns were only expressing a common attitude. Millions of people have given Communism their total loyalty, but Catholic isolationism sneers at any effort to understand and explain why Communism has been able to capture people's imaginations in the way it has. For American Catholic isolationists, the motives that prompted Julius and Ethel Rosenberg to go to their deaths as martyrs remain a closed book in which they are not even interested. Yet without some understanding of such conduct, the battle against Communism will be hard to win.

Discussion of Communism and the simple solution brings one to Senator McCarthy. If General MacArthur is a hero to the Catholic isolationists, Senator McCarthy is their knight on a white horse. There are American Catholics who support McCarthy because of a conviction that the Democratic Administration was unduly slow about moving against security risks. Members of this group do not take McCarthy lock, stock, and barrel, but tend to look on him as a kind of necessary nuisance, not without fault but able to keep attention focused on eliminating subversives from sensitive government posts. In my opinion, however, the hard core of Catholic support for McCarthy comes from the essentially isolationist, nativist wing, and has the same emotional roots as support for Father Coughlin had in the '30s. For the genuine isolationists among American Catholics, Joe McCarthy gives voice to all the frustrations, inadequacies, and contradictions that pull them in opposite directions. Although somewhat spotty, his voting record is predominantly isolationist. Like the Catholic isolationists, he has no coherent position. Like them, he is more *anti* than *pro,* and he shares their chronic inability to distinguish between the nonconformist and the Communist, between the liberal and the totalitarian, between the reformer and the revolutionist. But he does distract them from worry about why Communism was able to win the loyalties of millions of Chinese; he can keep the big problems small and the solutions simple, giving the impression that all our worries will be over "when the State Department is cleaned out," or Dean Acheson is gone, or George Marshall has retired, or perhaps soon, when John Foster Dulles has followed Acheson into political limbo.

In truth, Communism is capitalizing on the misery in which most of the world's people live. It feeds on hunger, it grows fat on the West's record of racial exploitation of the non-white peoples, and often it enlists its most dedicated disciples from the ranks of those who tired of waiting for the con-science of Christians to attack the wrongs of the world. It cannot be stressed too often that Communism did not create these problems, which would exist to plague the world if Marx had never been born. Instead, Communism takes advan-tage of the existing situation; because it can do so, the ter-rible danger exists that the exploited people of the world will be lured from one form of serfdom into another.

These are facts whose consequences Catholic isolationism refuses to face. Granting their truth would involve admitting that an eventual triumph over Communism will require infi-nitely more than security against internal subversion and espionage. The moral reform of which the world stands in need involves, among other things, the will to work and sac-rifice for the creation of a just social order all over the world. The war against poverty, disease, and ignorance is a just war, in which the Christian must be enlisted. More than that, in these times it is a war of survival. Millions will not go hungry forever when the leavings from our table would feed them. Avoiding the positive by concentrating almost exclusively on security measures means marking time on the sidelines while the Communists steal the big show.

It is in this area, I think, that Senator McCarthy's principal danger to the nation lies. The threat he represents is twofold. He has the traditional instinctive contempt of the demagogue for democratic processes, not in the sense that he is afraid of the people but precisely because he is confident of his ability to use them. He is supremely sure that he can turn the people into a mob. Such conduct can only pollute the wellsprings of American democratic life, at a time when we can least afford it.

In addition, Senator McCarthy has consistently demonstrated a very narrow and limited approach to the subject of Communism, for all his fame as an anti-Communist. If McCarthy could be a minor attraction, keeping attention focused on the need for internal security, perhaps those who give him limited support could make a case. But this is the purest kind of dreaming. McCarthy is apparently constitutionally incapable of staying on the sidelines, and the record shows that McCarthyism is much like pregnancy—there is no such thing as a small touch of it.

In practice, whatever the theory, McCarthy followers almost to a man seem to see the problem of Communism only in the narrow compass of their mentor and hero. Some halfhearted apologists for the Wisconsin Senator now argue that anti-McCarthyites have made too much of him and that McCarthyism is merely a sideshow. There is a certain modicum of truth in this claim: McCarthy *is* a sideshow; the problem is to keep him one, in order to preserve some sanity in our foreign policy.

For the typical Catholic isolationist, such criticisms of Senator McCarthy amount to *lèse-majesté*. Enthusiasm for him has become identified in their minds with both Americanism and Catholicism, and woe to the man who ventures to criticize. Here, in the manner in which they deal with those who do not share their attitudes on foreign policy, or—since the two are inextricably linked today—who cannot endorse their approach to "fighting Communism," the worst side of Catholic isolationism appears.

Catholic authorities generally say that the social encyclicals have much more authority than many Catholics are willing to concede, and I should think the papal statements on international order would carry much the same weight. Even so, rational discussion, study of the facts and figures, and calm exchange of ideas would seem preferable to beating isolationists over the head with papal pronouncements. But there is little question of that, if only for lack of opportunity.

Catholic isolationists in positions of influence do not say they disagree with the popes on such and such a point, for such and such a reason. Instead, after saying "aye, aye" to papal statements, they flout them in editorials, columns, and public talks. And then, to cap it all, they frequently have the supreme gall to couch their isolationist remarks in Catholic terms, to bedeck their nativist-nationalist positions with verbiage borrowed from Catholic social thought. And despite the fact that their general attitude on such matters is sharply at odds with the entire modern tradition of Catholic thought on international affairs, they never hesitate to use phrases like "so-called Catholics," "allegedly Catholic," "ostensibly Catholic," and the like to characterize those whose views they do not share. Once it was the Catholic who cited papal teaching on the family wage, or race, or labor unions, whose orthodoxy and personal character were questioned. Today, in my opinion, efforts to apply papal thought to international affairs produce a similar reaction.

In this era, the normal American isolationist, however sincere, represents a danger to the country. However good his motives, the Catholic isolationist in a position of power is doubly dangerous. He is a threat to the safety and welfare of the U.S. and hence to the peace of the world, and at the same time he seriously compromises the Church by giving the impression—intentionally or not—that his type of purely negative anti-Communism and isolationist thinking represents the Catholic point of view. Nothing could be further from the truth.

Ed Marciniak

CATHOLICS AND
SOCIAL REFORM

O NE OF the mature developments in American Catholic life is the movement for social reform. The history of the movement, as well as most contemporary manifestations of it, bears witness to this fact.

During the last decades of the nineteenth century, American Catholic interest was not, by and large, prompted by a social philosophy. By following the main currents of public opinion, Catholics hoped to make the Church respectable and "American" and to ward off more persecution of the Know-Nothing kind. Cardinal Gibbons brought this first period to an end in 1887 with his famous trip to Rome. In an unprecedented move he sought to have the Congregation of the Holy Office lift its condemnation against a U.S. labor organization, the Knights of Labor. And he succeeded.

The publication in 1891 of Leo XIII's encyclical *On the Condition of Labor,* stimulated partly by Cardinal Gibbons's persuasive support of U.S. workingmen, ushered in a second stage in the Catholic social movement. Now its aim was to reform, in the light of Christian social principles, the evils of industrial society. It presented an alternative to the reform proposals of the socialists who reached the peak of their influence in the early 1900's. In the writings of Monsignor John A. Ryan, starting with his *A Living Wage* in 1906, in the efforts of Father Peter Dietz to mobilize Catholic organizations for social reform, in the lay pioneers of the German Catholic Central *Verein* who prodded the Catholic social conscience, a Christian program was formulated for overhauling capitalism.

The era reached its climax in 1919. In that year the bishops of the United States set up the Social Action Department of the National Catholic Welfare Conference, with Monsignor Ryan as director, and issued the now famous *Bishops' Program of Social Reconstruction.* This declaration, reading in retrospect like a handbook of the New Deal, called for: minimum wage laws; comprehensive social insurance for illness, unemployment, and old age; laws against child labor; public employment services; government protection of the right to organize; co-operatives; government regulation of monopolies; graduated income, excess profit and inheritance taxes; sharing by workers in profits, ownership, and management; and public housing.

Then came the third and current stage in Catholic social action. Its chief influences were the great depression of the 1930's, Pius XI's 1931 encyclical, *Reconstructing the Social Order,* the founding of the *Catholic Worker* and of the Association of Catholic Trade Unionists, the establishment of Catholic labor schools across the country, the writings of men like Father Paul Hanly Furfey and the late Dom Virgil Michel, the efforts of Father Raymond McGowan, Father John P. Monaghan, Monsignor Reynold Hillenbrand and many others. Out of this social ferment came a deepened vision of a Christian view of society, recalling the redemptive, incarnational mission of the Mystical Body of Christ in each generation. As a result those in the Catholic social movement today find their credentials not only in U.S. citizenship or union membership, for example, but also in the sacraments of baptism and confirmation. We draw the spirit for our social reform not only from the cries of the poor and oppressed but also from the liturgy, Christ's sacrifice, which is the prime source of the Christian spirit.

It is a mark of the Catholic social movement's maturity that this religious deepening of its social spirit did not encourage sectarianism. Actually it promoted joint action among Catholics, Protestants, and Jews. In few areas of American life has there been more cordiality and less suspicion among religious-minded men than in the field of social reform. The reason for this intercreedal good will is clear, says Father John LaFarge, S.J.: "Catholic social action, in its different manifestations, has made perhaps the most marked impression upon the non-Catholic world of any form of Catholic activity during the last few years, chiefly because it grappled with problems in which non-Catholics are already deeply interested."

Testimony similar to Father LaFarge's would be volunteered by non-Catholic leaders in social action. For example, the Protestant writer Stanley Stuber in his *Primer on Roman Catholicism for Protestants* says: "If anyone is inclined to feel that the Roman Catholic Church is reactionary, he should examine its position in regard to social and economic matters. It has pioneered in labor relations, both in principle and practice, for over half a century. . . ." During the aftermath of World War II, Protestants, Jews, and Catholics pooled their views to draft four declarations: *Pattern for Peace* (an international world order), *Pattern for Economic Justice* (on economic reform), *Man's Relation to the Land* (on rural life), and *Human Relations in Modern Business* (on the responsibility of employers). Less formal statements were issued on anti-Semitism, fair employment practices, public housing, and other social questions.

Furthermore, when Monsignor (later Bishop) Francis J. Haas became a full-time chairman of the President's Fair Employment Practices Committee or when Monsignor John Boland was named full-time chairman of the New York State Labor Relations Board, no one demanded, in the name of the separation of Church and State, that the priests remove their clerical collars before seating themselves at their government desks. They were not forced to give up their jobs as were nuns who resigned as public-school teachers when school boards began requiring them to doff their religious dress.

Not only will it be possible, I hope, to conserve this area of mutual trust but also to extend it. No real progress in social reform is possible without the unstinting co-operation of all men of good will; the tasks of economic, political, and international reconstruction are of heroic proportions.

Traditional Catholic opinion has it that the Natural Law is the great unifying force. But our experience in social reform demonstrates the opposite. Our bond of unity with non-Catholics is not the Natural Law. It is charity. The issues that revolve around an understanding of the Natural Law—censorship, gambling, government-in-education, birth control, divorce, prostitution, for example—are those that generate the greatest disagreement. On the other hand, we have found common ground with other men of good will in the tension of preventing a race riot, in the heartaches of providing homes for the poor, in helping displaced persons and migratory workers, and in the daily comradeship of social action.

126

Catholics and Social Reform

Social action by Catholics matured with the realization that its object is the "salvation" of social institutions. The human person is part of, and influenced by, his culture, neighborhood, occupation, leisure-time pursuits, social status, the theater, the press, and government. The humanization and Christianization of these social institutions is now the recognized duty of the reformer. In arriving finally at such a conception of our role we have had to resist two undeniably attractive temptations.

The first temptation came when we were told that personal reform is more important than social reform, as though one is opposed to or excludes the other. When, for example, an influential figure like Bishop Fulton J. Sheen writes, "It is a few saints rather than social crusaders that we need," is it any surprise that the temptation to forsake social reform is so appealing? I am sure Bishop Sheen believes that social reform is not opposed to personal reform. What the world needs, certainly, is saints, and among them saintly social crusaders. "One cannot be a saint and live the Gospel we preach," Cardinal Suhard said, "without spending oneself to provide everyone with the housing, employment, goods, leisure, education, etc., without which life is no longer human."

The second temptation arose when we were told to evaluate our work in social reform by the converts it produces. But adopting such an attractive but ulterior motive as proselytizing makes it difficult for us to join in free and friendly collaboration to humanize social institutions. Honest collaboration demands purity of purpose if reforms are to be accomplished. How can a Catholic who is primarily interested in finding converts, and only incidentally in interracial justice, sit down honestly and work effectively with Jews and Protestants to discuss ways of banishing Jim Crow from medical

127

institutions? Wouldn't he be in the same position as a Jesuit seismologist who, after attending a scientific convention, would be required by his superiors to file a report on the number of conversions he made?

It is a great achievement of the Catholic social movement that it has rendered to laymen the things of laymen and to priests the things of priests. Social reform belongs pre-eminently, though not exclusively, to laymen, while religious formation is the priestly task. The lag in social teaching during the last century would never have occurred had laymen been given their place in the life of Christianity and had Christianity been given its place in their public life. The 1891 encyclical *On the Condition of Labor,* issued more than forty years after *The Communist Manifesto* of 1848, might have been written much earlier if laymen had understood better their role as citizens and as Christians. For when laymen by-passed Christianity in their public life, Western society was emptied of its soul: Christ. When Christianity by-passed laymen in its liturgical, apostolic, and educational life, Christianity was emptied of its social content.

In the formation of social-minded laymen the priest occupies a central place—as our experience with specialized groups like Young Christian Workers, the Christian Family Movement, and others indicates. Unless small groups of laymen are brought together to perfect themselves as citizens and as Christians, Christianity will withdraw even further from the world's market places, the arts and letters, the legislature, the news room, and the school. What a radical transformation of social institutions would ensue if most of the nation's forty-five thousand priests met regularly with small groups for intensive superstructural social—not political—growth.

The "salvation" of today's institutions, as the Catholic social movement recognizes, demands witnesses much more than apologists. Witnesses who will reveal the Christian mystery, whole and undefiled, by their devoted service in the political party, trade association, medical society, union, or community organization. Witnesses who will not withdraw from the workaday world. Witnesses who will stay to help redeem it.

Such an approach was, I feel, behind Pope Pius XII's granting Catholics the world over permission to eat meat last year on Friday, May Day (a labor holiday in most countries). Despite a few raised eyebrows among Catholics, the Pope's action represented no break with tradition. The Church has usually tried to Christianize secular celebrations rather than eliminate them. There are, of course, some who prefer to pressure police commissioners into banning May Day parades. But the Christian witness, picking up Pius XII's lead, will try to lift the joy, the spectacle, and the celebration of May Day Godwards.

However, not everything about the Catholic social movement rates a cheer. There is still a great deal of ignorance among Catholics regarding the Church's social doctrine. The average workingman knows little or nothing of the Christian teaching on a living wage, social legislation, or the dignity of manual labor. Nor is it unusual to find Catholic workers, after a talk on the social encyclicals, asking: "Why haven't we heard about these things before?" There are northern neighborhoods solidly populated by Catholics who never hear that racial segregation is immoral. There are suburban Catholics whose views on the United Nations echo more faithfully the Chicago *Tribune*'s isolationism than the Holy Father's keen awareness of the nations' interdependence.

Much has happened to dull the Catholic social conscience since the Depression '30s. The social and economic status of

American Catholics has improved rapidly. There are more middle-class Catholics than ever. The ordinary layman usually doesn't appreciate how vital is his active participation in movements for reform. And the conviction is widespread that social reform is the special function of the "labor priest," the social worker, the union leader, the legislator, or the "lay apostle." With a few notable exceptions, Catholic colleges do little to furnish leadership for social reform. And most of the large schools of commerce seldom turn out graduates who hope to rebuild the social system. Even the remarkable growth of social awareness in the Catholic press has been unable to halt the drift to the right.

Even where we have made progress in teaching Christian social doctrine, we frequently interpret and apply that teaching without imagination. Instead of using a social encyclical as a starting point for creative thinking and social reform, we use it as a terminal point. We frequently utter no word, express no thought that cannot explicitly be found in some papal document. The effects of this sterile approach are reflected in our discussions of the "industry council plan." Since Pius XI first outlined this plan for reconstructing the social order, how many original applications have we made to the specialized economic problems of the United States? As commentators, some of us rehash Pius XI's ideas without developing them. Others of us emasculate his thought by forever preaching his "principles," but never applying them to the concrete and particular. Is it any wonder that some of our expositions of papal social teaching have been characterized as "pious papal prattle"?

We fail to understand that in an encyclical the Holy Father records and gives authority to a development in social teaching that must usually establish itself first in open debate and discussion. The social reformer must not only follow the encyclicals; he must also precede them. "Pioneers," Cardinal Suhard once said, "will be forgiven for making mistakes." Unfortunately, many of the mistakes by Catholics have seldom been on the side of an imaginative and creative approach to new problems. Our reactions have suffered from a conformity to familiar and hackneyed patterns.

During the last decade Catholic organizations along occupational lines—for policemen, post-office employees, retail clerks, white-collar workers, firemen, doctors, newspaper people, railroad men, and others—have multiplied phenomenally. Our recognition of the need for associations of the occupational type is a welcome advance. But the centripetal direction of most such groups, with their *exclusive* emphasis on Communion breakfasts, holy hours, and similar religious practices, blocks the drive against secularism, and hence for social reform. The Christianization of economic institutions also requires centrifugal action, directing attention outward to the moral problems of the trade, office, industry, or profession. I do not plead for Catholic blocs in the trades or professions; rather I hope that existing Catholic organizations will increasingly become centers for moving laymen to judge the problems of their occupational environment in the light of the Gospel.

Finally, we sometimes overlook the fact that American opinion tends to be cynical about do-gooders in general and about social reformers in particular. It expects to find a hidden "angle" or vested interest in apparently unselfish causes. And it loves nothing better than to expose some do-gooding faker.

Public reaction to civic action by Catholics partakes of this cynicism, but it is also suspicious of a vested political motive.

If we keep this fact in mind, we may avoid the habit of speaking out only on public issues with a Catholic interest, narrowly conceived, like birth control or aid to education. One eastern Holy Name Society, silent all the years of its existence, broke silence this year with a protest against legal action being taken to ban bingo.

On the other hand several Catholic groups this year actively supported civic measures designed to aid and improve public schools. Such action generates a climate for the co-operation of all men of good will in social reform. For no real progress in social reform is possible without the unstinting co-operation of Protestants, Jews, and Catholics. The tasks of economic, political, and international reconstruction are of heroic proportions. I pray that men of religious convictions will try, even at great personal sacrifice, to extend the common ground of social action.

Ed Willock

CATHOLIC RADICALISM
IN AMERICA

T HE LIMITS of Catholic orthodoxy are far more extensive than are ever explored by the average parochial society. The outposts of Catholicism are farther flung than could be realized by those who regard the all too apparent manifestations of ghetto sectarianism as intrinsic to the faith rather than (as they are) a historical accident of immigrant Europeanism. Since the turn of the century a tradition has been in the making among Catholics that is characterized by a return to a more literal interpretation of the Gospels, a repugnance for the sort of Christianity that canonizes the familiar and damns the strange. The new tradition attempts to bring together in the same bed such strangers as religious contemplation and social consciousness.

A race of "radical" Catholics has sprung up and is now in its second generation. Its (happily) unorganized membership can be numbered in thousands. Though characteristic emphasis has been placed by this group upon lay initiative, there are perhaps (proportionately) more priests in its company than laymen (a fact that indicates to me that the "clericalism" which so many bewail is less a matter of clerical imposition than one of immature apron-clinging by the laity).

Although this movement may be recognized by the unconventionality of its ideas, it is by no means merely a new ideology. A failure to grasp this point has caused all sorts of
mistakes. Since the birth of printing and the vaunted Age of
Reason the world has been the playground for innumerable
garret philosophies. The theme has been essentially doctrinaire with social overtones. The strategy of being antiacademy
saved few of these garret philosophers from the fate of being
academic. The radical Catholicism of which I speak has its
roots in no school of thought but rather in a renewal of Christian sympathy for the massed victims of industrial society.
Though one may trace certain similarities between the ideas
and approaches of radical Catholics in this country and Catholic movements in Europe, the similarity cannot be traced
scholastically but is due simply to the common faith finding
itself immersed in the same social difficulties. By way of illustration I cite an incident back in 1937.

The place was Boston, in the front room of the Catholic
Worker House of Hospitality. Peter Maurin, the cofounder of
the Catholic Worker movement, was visiting us during a speaking tour of the New England area. One of "the boys," obviously
on the bum, had just entered off the street. He mumbled something about wanting a bite to eat. Peter looked up from the
book he had been reading, pulled off his glasses, and muttered,
"Wait here." He left the room. A moment later he returned
and told the man he could go downstairs and have some grub.
The beggar was profuse in his thanks. Peter lifted two flutter-
ing hands in a Gallic gesture and said, "No, no, no! I must
thank *you!*" He darted us all a glance to see that we were
attentive and shouted aloud: "Point!" For those of us who
knew him this cry of attention was not unlike a French ma-

gician's *"Voilà!"* It meant simply: "Now watch, this is it! Here
is an idea to be remembered! This is the point."

For the benefit of everyone present Peter announced clearly:
"I can give you bread and meat" (directing his words to the
guest, who stood blinking) "and coffee. Yes, I can give you
these—but *you?* YOU" (tapping the fellow on his shirt front)
"give me the chance to practice Christian charity. You are an
ambassador of God. Thank you!" His point was made.

The Catholic Worker Houses of Hospitality, of which there
were as many as forty scattered among the larger American
cities, have been centers of radical Catholicism for over
twenty years. The ramifications of this point made by Peter
Maurin explain the perspective peculiar to the radical Catholic, a perspective rather than a *summa,* doctrine, or party
line.

Consider how contrary to prevailing norms of social service
is this notion that the worker, the volunteer, is the object of
reform rather than the poor. What a reversal of values, especially for Americans, who are noted the world over as a nation
of evangelical busybodies intent upon "saving" everyone! During every moment of its existence the Catholic Worker has
collided head-on with the criticism: "But what good do you
do these bums, these drunks?" The only answer in the light
of the Catholic Worker philosophy is that the House of Hospitality exists not to "do good" to its guests but to feed, clothe,
and house them. It exists before this for the moral reform of
those who voluntarily live among and serve Christ in His poor.

The revolutionary implication of this new approach to
"charity" may not be immediately obvious. So let's consider it
further. Unlike most workers among the poor, the volunteers
in the Catholic Worker movement feel no *divine* compulsion
to "convert" the down and out, to reassimilate him into the

elect society from which he has become alienated due to his nastiness. They feel no conviction that they are the ambassadors of the good life, bringing Jesus to the Bowery. On the contrary, the Bowery brings Jesus to them. They are in no way prepared to inculcate mores of "respectability," to champion the cause of bourgeois virtue, to resist the tendency to "go native." They live among the poor and the outcast in order to be *themselves* the victims. Thus, you see, their "righteous" defenses are down, and it becomes inevitable that rather than winning they themselves will be won over. There is an *esprit de corps* among *les misérables* that is mighty infectious. The poor have an alarmingly candid perspective on society. One can never be overly impressed by the social façade once one has seen what lies behind. Herein is the explanation of the radical Catholic social perspective.

The people in the Catholic Worker movement came to see society from the bottom up, that is, from the person up to the institution. They saw the Hotel Metropole from the kitchen and the employees' locker room. They saw the steel industry from beside the blast furnaces and from under the striker's placard. They saw the World's Fair through the eyes of the day workers who clawed the swampy flats and dug the holes out of which the wonders of the world would grow; they saw these same donkey laborers expelled when their work was finished and then driven out of New York in order to clean up the streets in preparation for the incoming visitors. They saw the ocean liners from the crew's quarters, and the agricultural industry from the sharecroppers' shacks. They saw all these things because they went among the poor, not to save but to be saved.

The Catholic Worker people actually committed that frightful sin of becoming emotionally involved with their "cases."

When they heard of a place where Negroes were ostracized they went with their placards to court the same disfavor. Who was dirty, outcast, spurned, and they were not dirty, outcast, and spurned? This identification of themselves with the poor and oppressed explains many of their techniques (or lack of techniques) and most of their doctrines.

Catholicism of the conservative variety retains the anachronistic medieval perspective that allies itself with princes and principles, with law and order, with holy hearth and the closed parish. The Catholic Worker's permissive approach to the socially outcast afforded Catholics a view closer to the stocks than to the judgment seat. The betrayal of princes, the inadequacy of principles, the abuses of law, and the preference of order to justice became more apparent. Other doctrines were emphasized. A man is measured less by his orthodoxy than by his potential membership in the Mystical Body of Christ. A man is a sacred vessel, no matter how lowly he may be, much more sacred in fact than ecclesiastical pots and pans. Christ is recognized as Victim in the outcast, the ostracized, the unemployable; the emphasis is placed there rather than in His sojourn among the elect. The Oneness of all mankind in charity became more significant than our several interpretations and denials of Revealed Truth.

The impact of the Catholic Worker, the penny paper and the movement that grew out of it, on the American Catholic body as a whole is immediately shocking but yet, in its long-range effect, subtle. It has been, as intended, a leavening influence and consequently at its mature stage not readily isolated from the whole dough. This efficacy, of which we now have evidence, is the proof of the genius and the essential holiness of Dorothy Day and Peter Maurin, its founders. Two characterizations which to many appeared to be aberrations contributed greatly to the efficacy of this movement. The first was bluntness and unconventionality carried to the point of being shocking. The second was an abhorrence of organization and "looking for results." These two policies stand in glaring contrast to the usual tactful diplomacy of approach coupled with hyper-organization and closely tabulated scoring.

The *Catholic Worker* made no bones about where it stood on such unpopular questions as pacifism, neutralism toward the Spanish War, love of the Communist, full acceptance of the Negro, the spiritual semitism of Catholics, disgust at Catholic affluence, and distrust of industrial capitalism. Peter Maurin blasted complacent Catholics to their faces and Dorothy Day demanded the furs of the well-to-do be given to clothe her cherished poor. Nuances may have been overloaded, but the point was always made. Had it been quieter or less rowdy, radical Catholicism could not have survived. In a day of mealymouthed clichés, the *Catholic Worker* spoke simply yeas and nays.

Had the Catholic Worker organized its membership, its size and scope would have been obviously formidable. Had it tabulated the results of its charities and social influence, the statistics would have been staggering. (For example, in one large city a group compiled figures which indicated that of every dollar given to the community chest, ten cents reached the poor; whereas in the Catholic Worker more than ninety-nine cents of a donated dollar was spent directly upon the needy.) Yet to what avail this show of strength? With organization the Catholic Worker would have gained a national prestige and "respectability" that would have damned it in the eyes of those among whom it labored. It might have become another organization.

Look around and count the aged, the useless, and the ob-

solete institutions that continue to exist thanks to nothing else
but the excellence of their organizational structure. Organizational techniques have been perfected in our time to insure the
perpetuation of institutions that otherwise might have entered
an early and well-deserved grave. The Catholic Worker came
into being to bring about a change of heart. All its conferences,
works of mercy, and rural experiments were only means to
this end. It must have succeeded to some degree in this reformation, otherwise how explain its survival? It took none of the
usual steps to perpetuate itself (organization, budgeting, self-
definition, establishment of prestige through controlled press
relations, flattering affluent people, cautious administration,
etc.).

From its beginning the Catholic Worker has tottered on the
brink of disaster. When its houses were penniless and in debt
it continued to espouse wholly unpopular causes in utter defiance of every law of survival except trust in divine providence. It is almost certain that this foolhardiness has been the
Catholic Worker's key to survival. This madness testified (no
matter how obtuse the observer might be) to the fact that the
thing that made it tick was something mysterious, other-
worldly, which existed in defiance of human logic and strategy.
Talk though one may (and who has not?) about preferable
techniques of operation, better ways of helping the worker,
more effective methods of clarification, it is doubtful if a better
way could be devised to accomplish the specific result intended
by the founders.

The quantitative influence of the Catholic Worker cannot
be calculated. Its qualitative influence can only be felt. I have
felt it. When in company with three other laymen I founded
Integrity magazine back in 1946, we established a policy that
made us dependent for our very survival upon the efficacy of

Catholic Worker indoctrination. We counted heavily upon the fact that the movement's ideas had caught on. We appealed to a Catholic audience on a national scale, and the generous response was a surprise even to us. Had not the ground been prepared for us, the plea of *Integrity* for self-criticism by American Catholics would have been laughed out of existence. *Integrity* yet survives, and with each passing year it experiences the abundant fruit of seed sown by the Catholic Worker. Those who doubt the Catholic Worker completely are few. Yet, those who have been untouched by it are fewer. Repelled by certain inevitable traces of Bohemia and fanaticism (inevitable in a movement that prefers persons to institutions) thousands have disassociated themselves from the Catholic Worker only to carry their leaven into more organized and conservative areas of society.

The influence of the Catholic Worker on the American Church though seldom found in a concentrated form leaves significant traces in almost every parish. There are places now, for example, where Catholics are ashamed of their luxury, where priests waive all title to clerical privilege, where churches are simply and beautifully decorated, where parishioners participate in liturgical ceremonies, where race discrimination is regarded as an abomination, where religious convictions animate social reform, where college graduates prefer manual labor, where Catholics of talent and genius remain to serve rather than chase after money. Such places are legion.

With all this (as with all human movements), the Catholic Worker has its weakness. Its very abhorrence of organization is a guarantee of a certain ineffectuality in social areas where organized co-operation is of the essence. Some of these are the family, the school, the community, the productive enterprise, and the political order. An over-preoccupation with personal autonomy (even in a day when the pendulum has swung far to the other side) can blind one to the essentiality of an organized social order and consequent loyalties to authority and the common good. *Integrity,* though a magazine rather than a movement, while rejoicing in the radical tradition, has placed most of its emphasis upon the relation between personal virtue and the demands of social co-operation.

Take the family for example. *Integrity* has stressed certain aspects of family life which, were they to be generally adopted, would have a far more profound influence upon society and the spirits of men than, let us say, the nationalization of steel or granting organized labor a share in management. One such would be, for example, the readoption by Catholics of the ideal of a large family. Another would be a restoration to the family father of a sense of Christian vocation. The first of these would have a profound influence in the direction of decentralization, living standards that would include children, domestic architecture, and the glorification of the matron rather than the model. The second would re-establish the family as being a social entity at least as deserving of esteem and consideration as a business enterprise. It could also result in the family's having as much representation in our legislatures as is now enjoyed, for example, by oil, steel, breakfast cereals, railroads, and financial houses.

Radical Catholicism in America has profited greatly from the more mature movements of a similar nature in Europe. It is my conviction, however, that in the past decade the American brand has moved considerably away from slavish imitation and is well on the way to evolving mystiques and techniques more compatible with the native climate.

I have mentioned here only one movement and one magazine, the Catholic Worker and *Integrity*. It would be easy to mention more, but once to begin the list would make it quite difficult to stop. The radical impetus feathers out in so many directions that one is never sure where precisely it ceases to be the predominant color and conservatism begins.

But one other movement do I dare mention as properly fitting into the radical category. That is the Friendship House movement. This is a sister movement to the Catholic Worker, paralleling it in many respects but limiting its main concern to Negro-white relationships. Here we find again the highly significant immersion of the volunteer in the same difficulties as the sufferer. Above all, the workers at Friendship House bear witness to their disgust at segregation by setting up their houses and living in colored areas of large cities. Rather than extend lily-white hands across racial fences, they move right in and join the colored community. This form of bearing witness to a conviction, year after year, in spite of the obvious gargantuan proportions of the problem, is a technique as ancient as Christianity and the sort of foolhardy thing most likely to bring about profound reform.

Joseph E. Cunneen

CATHOLICS AND
EDUCATION

Is it possible at this time even to begin a serious examination of the interaction between Catholicism and American education? If the widespread response to the brand of criticism associated with the name of Paul Blanshard continues to make us Catholics feel that we are the victims of a new wave of bigotry, we may be missing an opportunity for profitable examination of conscience in regard to both parochial and public education. When we hear naïvely doctrinaire enthusiasts of the public schools make implicitly totalitarian statements on education, or on the desirability of compulsory attendance at such schools, or on starving private schools into submission, what is our answer to be?

Must our response intensify those tendencies that encourage an isolationist American Catholicism? Are we to take an unhealthy secret pleasure in these attacks, since they confirm us in our assurance that we alone have been right all the time? Is the situation to be an excuse for a counterattack on the public schools, with the usual Catholic barrage against John Dewey and progressive education?

The level of our reply is important, for although it is hard to see why Mr. Blanshard himself should be considered more intellectually respectable than earlier Know-Nothings, many of those who have somehow found in him a distorted echo of their own fears about Catholicism are asking very real questions, and are motivated by praiseworthy religious, ethical, and democratic ideals. It might be helpful if we tried to understand why men who should not be truly considered anti-Catholic are fearful of what they consider generally held Catholic attitudes in education. The sincerity and seriousness of their concern recall the accurate observation of Cardinal Gibbons (made in a letter to Pope Leo XIII, December 30, 1890) that divisions between American Catholics and their fellow citizens "are caused above all by the opposition against the system of national education which is attributed to us, and which, more than any other thing, creates and maintains in the minds of the American people the conviction that the Catholic Church is opposed by principle to the institutions of the country and that a sincere Catholic cannot be a loyal citizen of the United States."

Many Catholics themselves have long been dissatisfied with certain aspects of Catholic education as it now exists. However, if, like this writer, they are loyal graduates of Catholic grammar school, high school, college, and graduate school, they are naturally reluctant to make their discontent public, especially at a time when parochial schools seem to be under fire. But in some respects the greatest harm done to Catholicism by its bigoted critics could be to slow up the necessary and barely begun process of self-criticism in all areas of Catholic life. Serious Catholic examination of our own schools tends to be divided between realistic appraisal of the need to continue raising standards at all levels, and the discouraged recognition that our graduates, although steady churchgoers, often have a passive, formalistic, and moralistic conception of their membership in the Church. It is generally recognized that the lack of funds is not the only problem.

When one considers the paternalistic priest-layman relationship that naturally developed among poor and leaderless groups, and the necessity of insuring a rough-and-ready survival before even the most elementary educational problems could be tackled, no apologies are needed in any comparison between parochial and public schools. The really surprising thing is not that teaching nuns may have fewer semester hours of credit in "Methods of Education" than their public-school counterparts, but that this unique and immense system of Catholic institutions, from primary to graduate school, was instituted in so short a time by an immigrant population at the bottom of the American economic ladder. Anyone making generalized assumptions about the inferior quality of Catholic schools in America should be asked to present reasonable evidence and criteria. We Catholics of the younger generation especially should not underrate the accomplishment of our fathers in building the school system. If today the academic standards of earlier years seem to be inadequate—if we find a textbook still explaining literature in essentially philistine terms, or an aged religion teacher stubbornly repeating that the world is 5,853 years old—it might be chastening to ask ourselves if we have as instinctive a Christian sense as our fathers in the face of such things as birth and death, poverty, work, and respectability, sin and the love of God.

Responsible Catholic critics who are working for higher standards feel that training in the technique of learning, as well as disinterested top-level scholarship, suffers from the understandable but misguided desire to have the educational content itself provide the direct motives for piety. There is sometimes an insufficient awareness of what an ambiguous thing it is to teach the love of God. Such teaching is made even more precarious when in a particular sociological and psychological context the wrong answer can mean expulsion from the group. Although the tendency to exaggerate the value of Catholic novels or the reliability of Catholic historians is happily decreasing, signs of an excessive and sometimes aggressive sense of our minority status are still much too prevalent.

Some Catholic parents and even school administrators betray by their attitudes that they are essentially indifferent to the positive value of general education. That secular knowledge is to be prized for its own sake, and is necessary for the Christian who is to consecrate himself to the work of civilization: these often seem only empty phrases.

Sometimes there is serious disagreement between those who are emphasizing the necessity of higher educational standards and those convinced that our schools are not Catholic enough. The latter feel, for example, that there are too many Catholic teachers of economics who would be flattered to be told that their courses—with the exception of a prayer before and after class—are identical with those offered at the Harvard School of Business Administration. They are right in pointing out that the class in religion at present is often only an extra chore for students of a Catholic grammar school, or that a scientific course in theology is not at present the central discipline of any existing Catholic university, that Catholic schools have sometimes paid too high a price for quick accreditation. The burden of our school system sometimes seems hardly worth carrying when one recognizes that the majority of our graduates know little about Catholic social thought, mental prayer, or intelligent participation in the official worship of the Church. However, those pleading for what they consider more distinctively Catholic institutions often betray a zealous but misguided desire to turn the existing schools into simple training centers for "Catholic Action."

When the quality of graduates is criticized, it soon becomes clear that the inadequacy of our schools is both part cause and part reflection of the level of American Catholicism in general. The process of religious erosion is going on, not only in some mechanistically oriented public-school classes in biology; it is present in even more frightening form in the collective yawn at the Mass attended—there are penalties for absence—by the entire student body of a Catholic school. In America today no wall, no complete system of Catholic Scout groups, CYO teams, sodalities, or clubs can keep out the evil with which we are concerned. It is already in the Chancery offices, in our concern for bigness, in our various compromises with racism, in our exaggerated respect for money, and in our eagerness for success.

It seems fairly evident that those who are working quietly for higher educational standards have produced more durable and positive results—whether by avoiding anti-Protestant polemics and pious euphemisms in explaining the background of the Reformation, or by carrying on further experimentation in judicious borrowing from "progressive education," along the lines of the elementary school textbooks sponsored by the Commission on American Citizenship at the Catholic University of America. Their work would be easier if the desire to expand the Catholic school system did not often operate automatically.

On the parish level, unless the people are very poor or very thinly spread out over a large area, the absence of a school is often taken to mean that the pastor is either lazy or a poor organizer. The planning and responsibility for opening a new parochial school might well utilize a competent board of professional educators. Such a board could advise the pastor—in the long run sparing both him and his parishioners many unhappy scenes—that just any building with nuns teaching in it is not necessarily preferable to the existing schools in the area; that it is a betrayal of the Church's legitimate concern for education to let her insistence be portrayed to the world as one that complacently accepts inferior facilities and lower academic standards in her desire that children be grounded in the catechism. If a new school is under construction, the question regarding the ability to pay for it ought to be put in terms which assume that the Catholic demand is for the best.

The unhappy effects of ignoring this rough wisdom are perhaps most apparent in higher education, where the fear of Catholic attendance at a state university sometimes causes a religious order to blind itself to the practical requirements of a college or university plant. That institution whose faculty is inadequately staffed (or inadequately paid), whose libraries and laboratories cannot fulfill the needs which the courses described in the catalogue demand, ought to have its very reason for existence questioned, and ought not to be able to hide behind those "sound Catholic principles" which it believes itself to be imparting.

The professional board of which we are in need would in one case tell the head of a religious order that he has neither the funds nor the qualified personnel to run a proposed new school, that the order ought not start another Catholic college simply because none exists in a particular area. On the other hand, the board might be equally insistent about other needs—the immediate desirability, for instance, of additional bilingual parochial grammar and high schools for the growing Puerto Rican population in New York. Although the parishes in which they are most numerous could not absorb the cost of these schools, there is no reason why the cost could not be borne by a diocesan or, if necessary, a national fund.

It is extremely unfortunate that we Catholic parents have, in the main, been encouraged to be passive—paying, but non-voting—members in a school system that is usually justified as a defense of our rights. We are grateful for the sacrifice of the teaching sisters, and try to support our schools generously, but we have a curiously ambiguous attitude toward them. We constantly complain about "money sermons" and "building pastors," and rarely think of the schools as our own. Though we are prepared to protest an alleged instance of bigotry on the part of a public-school teacher, we are far too little disposed to ask questions if one of our children comes back from a parochial-school class ready to accuse his non-Catholic playmates of all kinds of "mortal sins."

Although the necessity for the parochial system is never openly challenged, and is even proclaimed as the Catholic norm in all times and places, ominous reference to the "pain of mortal sin" is apparently necessary to keep many of us from choosing the public school or secular college for our children, even where Catholic institutions already exist. There would be a different attitude both within and without if attendance at Catholic schools had less of a compulsory character about it, and if the effective control over at least the majority of them—with due regard for the authority of the bishop —were in the hands of qualified laymen, the educational deputies of responsible and articulate parents. There would also be a different attitude in the parish if we learned to make our financial contribution to the school not as the obligatory and semigrudging discharge of an additional tax imposed by outside authorities, but as the responsible contribution toward the realization of unique requirements in education, over which control is exercised through an elected parish school board.

The middle-class suburb in which my family and I live may not be typical, but it affords a study of some of the problems in community relations involved in Catholic attitudes toward education. The Catholic population here was formerly quite small, but has recently grown to about 40 per cent. The building fund for the new church is well under way, and the pastor has made it clear that he considers this merely the first step in a fund-raising drive that will produce a school and convent.

The local public school seems to have and to deserve the general confidence of the community. Although some Catholic parents are exercising their rights by sending their children to Catholic schools, those who have children in the public school have no major complaint against it.

In such a relatively stable community it should not be impossible to get parents' positive co-operation in a program of religious education for the children, and even to use some of the undoubted good will that now exists to help Catholic parents bring up their children in the faith. The energy now expended by the Holy Name Society in disposing of chance books for the raffle of a $3,000 Buick is certainly greater than that needed to train them to be the nucleus in a parish dialogue or sung Mass, for instance. Various other ways could be found to make the common worship of the parish a potent method for the best kind of "modern" learning-by-doing. No effort in this direction has been made. On the contrary.

And although all sides piously proclaim that the school is above politics, in a small town so much of the annual budget is involved in the school that an election of a school board or a vote on the school budget can create rather ugly political divisions. In our town there has been a conspicuous alliance between Catholics prominent in parish organizations and groups such as the Taxpayers' Association whose thinking emphasizes concern for the tax rate and property values. The common enemy of this alliance? The public school. In election after election, although most of their children are now attending the school, these Catholics have been active in seeking to defeat the appropriation of funds for a school library, for additional classrooms, or in seeking to elect to the school board those who would reflect their views. Inevitably, ill feeling has been stirred up. Although the word "divisive" is rightly considered a special contribution to jargon by professional anti-Catholics, the Catholic response to the problem of education in our town gives it some meaning.

At a parish Holy Name meeting I attended there was a constant insistence that the bricks and mortar necessary for a Catholic building would cost less than those for a public school. There was the fallacious assumption that if one-third of the students in the public school were transferred to a parochial one, the school tax could be cut proportionately. The general disposition seemed to be to think of the Catholic school problem as if it existed in a vacuum. There was little awareness that no estimate for financing the Catholic school could be realistic if it did not allow for the inevitable increase in the over-all school population, both public and parochial, in the years just ahead.

No one asked if the creation of a parochial school in a town of our size might seriously injure the public school, and if so, how that might affect our Christian moral obligation. There was nothing said to indicate that religious education was needed by others than children. One man declared he would do all he could to see his daughter through Catholic grammar and high school; after that, if she did not turn out well, he would feel that at least he had done his duty.

The climax was reached when a successful young Catholic contractor made an emotional pledge of support for the future parochial school, saying, "I don't mind giving it [money] to you, Father, but I'll be damned if I give another cent to that damned Truman Administration!" There is no reason to believe that his attitude has been substantially altered by the change in Washington. What did he mean? I think he meant nothing less than that his understanding of Catholicism impels him to serve the common good only under duress, grudgingly, since it is a "secular" thing. But he is willing to close his eyes if it can be guaranteed to him that he is serving a Catholic organizational apparatus, which for him apparently has no obligation to the community at large. Under such circumstances, as a matter of conscience, I would have to vote against this type of Catholic candidate for the local school board.

Many who are not unfriendly critics of Catholicism would shake their heads on hearing the above account, and say, "Yes, that's the way it is." But such observers rarely have a hearing among us Catholics, who prefer to believe that only the godless, the invincibly ignorant, or the Protestant in the last stage of religious dissolution can have any real fear of the still-growing Catholic school system. Knowing of the precarious existence of our own schools, we find it hard to realize that public schools themselves need a helping hand these days. The fact is that in many cases the additional parochial school is a threat to the public school, in terms of both economic and moral support. Sometimes this threat is exaggerated, but it is made credible by what looks like Catholic co-operation with groups which, sometimes unintentionally, have served to undermine confidence in public schools from Pasadena to Scarsdale.

We are too fond of saying what a saving our schools are to the American taxpayer. It is undoubtedly true that in a crowded city whose educational facilities are already strained, pupils can be educated more cheaply in a parochial school than in a public school, thanks to the nuns' vow of poverty. Even here the "gift" to the city is not as absolute as we often represent it; the hidden economics involved in paying for the parochial school affects the entire community. There is only so much money available for education within a given area; money withdrawn for Catholic schools is being taken out of a potentially common fund. Some economy-minded Catholic members of large city boards of education make non-Catholics understandably skeptical about our boast of a gift to the taxpayer. Furthermore, in small towns, the addition of a Catholic school may mean a duplication of facilities that in fact is extremely uneconomical.

We are legitimately impatient with those philosophical monists whose fear of any co-operation between religion and education hides their desire to level all educational goals in terms of their own drably uniform conception of the ideal citizen. But are we not sometimes unaware of the semantic confusion current in the term "cultural pluralism"? If cultural pluralism is an un-American bugaboo in the sense that all doctrinal and ideological differences must be ironed out before genuine assimilation can be achieved, then Catholicism, too, is un-American. The editors of such a journal as the *Christian Century,* however, who cannot be considered indifferent to the problem of religious education, have something else in mind when they warn against pluralism.

They are asking whether the common good is not imperiled

if distinct and total social groupings are solidified in early and formative years, and if there is a tendency to carry over such groupings unduly even in later years, cutting straight through the social structure. The word "total" is important here. It is a positive value to be given a sense of one's personal religious heritage at specifically religious ceremonies and by doctrinal instruction. Insofar as such things are divisive, it is a reflection of real divisions that cannot be obscured. But it is quite a different thing always to play baseball or go camping or hear the abstract command to love your neighbor with no friends other than those of one's own religious faith present. How will the group experience of the students of a parochial school eventually merge with the community? Would it not be more logical for a Catholic child, reared in specifically Catholic institutions from parochial to graduate school, to be drafted into segregated "Catholic" divisions of the army, or serve on a "Catholic" warship or air wing?

It is not enough to say that Catholic schools teach love of one's neighbor and give the deepest moral and emotional sanction for this injunction. It is no answer to say that Catholic teachers—lay and religious—are individually and collectively patriotic. The fears of Catholic pluralism would not exist unless many of our graduates had been observed suffering from the ill effects of this total sociological conditioning.

American interest in theorizing is not high, and public awareness of intra-Catholic discussion on the problem of Church and State—*e.g.*, Ryan-Boland *vs.* Maritain-Murray—is almost negligible. Most of our non-Catholic neighbors know little about the thesis of the "Catholic State." They are all too aware, however, of Catholic-bloc mentalities that imply acceptance of this thesis in areas of "special interest"—Catholic attempts to control the public-school board, confused Catholic efforts to translate absolute standards of objective morality into specific, of necessity partially relativistic, legislation, etc. Some of our non-Catholic neighbors who are better educated in history cannot help being aware, too, that clerical control of education in many European countries was a prize in a struggle for power, fought with disastrous educational and national consequences that are still evident. They are right to wish to avoid such a struggle here in America.

At the present time somewhat more than half of the Catholic children in grammar school, high school, and college are attending Catholic schools. The Catholic "thesis," usually presented without qualification, is: "Every Catholic child in a Catholic school." Is this really to be our aim? Would it really be to the advantage of either the Church or of America to withdraw the other 50 per cent of Catholic students from public and secular schools? Would not Catholic participation in such schools, whether as administrators, teachers, or members of boards of education, be understandably resisted if we did so?

We must seriously ask ourselves if we can build up the Catholic school system indefinitely without doing major harm to the only practical American alternative. We cannot simply pay reverence to the Catholic "thesis" in behalf of a Christ-centered education; we should also take an honest look around to see in what way the American context may modify that thesis.

The reality of the economic situation is one of the things that modify it. It would be a sad thing for all concerned if the Catholic school system disintegrated from financial exhaustion, after long and bitter fights for public funds. It would be quite a different thing if Catholics, as a matter of free choice, confident in the religious vitality of Catholic homes and parishes, and in the possibility of creating reasonable safeguards for the faith of Catholics attending non-ideological public schools and colleges, worked for greater integration within the general educational structure. Many Catholics today are privately asking themselves if our present attempt in education is yielding a maximum return from the effort expended.

For example, many Catholic observers seem to feel that expansion in higher education is especially impractical, and its positive result would most often be superficial. They point to the increasingly prohibitive cost of equipment for college departments in science, and emphasize that students in certain areas should not be discouraged from attending secular universities whose facilities cannot be rivaled. Can we, however, adopt a policy that implies that it is "necessary" for students preparing to be lawyers to take their training under Catholic auspices, but that those who wish to be physicians must take their chances in a secular atmosphere?

As a matter of fact, isn't it a strange kind of economic planning that spends almost the entire Catholic educational effort on half its students, leaving the other half to feel that at best they are the victims of an unfortunate geographical location, and quite possibly shouldn't be attending the schools in which they find themselves? Don't we encourage a second-class Catholic status for those who are attending secular schools and colleges, and don't we often see this class distinction prolonged into later years: between those who are constantly within the official Catholic organizational order, and those who tend to be identified with the general community? (These groupings are not perfectly interchangeable.)

We hear many vague things about "leakage" caused by attendance at secular schools, but we fail to recognize that our attitude of grudging tolerance encourages the Catholic attending them to seek out a new loyalty. Is it really any help, for example, for a speaker at a Newman Club to expound exclusively on the advantages of Catholic colleges, and encourage a defensive and negative response to the genuine values to which these Catholic students will be introduced? Because of the purely negative approach of their earlier Catholic schooling, I have seen Catholic students in secular colleges, excited in their youthful idealism by getting a glimpse of a vocation of public service, come to feel that their loyalties were being divided, or that the new ideal had no place in the Catholic apparatus they had been supporting.

We Catholics in America do not reflect enough on the uniqueness of the experiment being conducted here, both politically and educationally. Public general education is still a new thing. Whatever its shortcomings, it has marked a great step forward. We may regret that the movement for public education emerged without a specific Catholic contribution, and at a time when American Protestantism was losing much of its vigor. It might also be said that, except for these conditions, this step might not have been made at all.

Certainly the assumptions of American public education, in many ways parallel to the assumptions of the American form of government, and the American tradition on Church and State, are such that Catholicism's European experiences offer no exact precedent. The thesis of the Catholic school, like the thesis of the "Catholic State," was really grounded in the assumption that all schools were religious, that the alternatives were Catholic schools or Protestant, Jewish, or pagan schools. The American government is committed to an exciting—and so far, fruitful—experiment in which the State is not ideologically or religiously committed. The State is neutral but not unfriendly toward religion.

Although education affects the whole man, it is misleading to say simply that it is a "sacral" activity. Catholics are not the only ones who understand that an education that keeps all mention of religion out of the curriculum is, in effect, telling the child that religion is unimportant, if not worse. If we are also aware of the arrogance of innovators in educational theory, we can understand how public education could come to teach a religion of secularism. Insofar as this is true, the public school is as guilty as the Catholic school of indoctrination, and dishonest to boot, since it does not represent fairly the education it is giving. At least to some extent we must believe that the public school today is a closed system, abandoning much of its educational responsibility for the sake of training its ideal "democratic citizen."

We would do well not to overstate this case. Few of our public educators are intentionally hostile to religion. If Catholics as well as others suspect that the public school today is not neutral, that it does not leave the atmosphere of the school open to the supernatural, but is rather closed within a facile self-sufficient optimism in which God is considered unnecessary, we must try to understand how this condition came about. The situation may be chiefly a reflection of dangerous general attitudes in America (from which Catholics are not exempt) in which the pride of a young and prosperous nation at the peak of its power may have gone to its head. But part of the responsibility for the secularism of the public schools may, ironically, be due to the existence of the parochial schools. "If people want that kind of education," the secularist could say, "let them go to such schools; let the public schools be for those that want the real thing." It is certainly true that the vaguely Protestant religious atmosphere of the public school has been diminishing as the Catholic school plant has grown.

Catholics and Education

No one but a lunatic would be in favor of closing all the Catholic schools tomorrow. But it may be the poorer strategy, all things considered, to point our efforts to the final goal of "every Catholic child in a Catholic school." It also seems economically impossible. Certainly, as long as our theoretical "ideal" remains that of duplicating religious school systems, non-Catholics—some with sorrow and some with anger—will not wish to aid us in the financing of our schools, and, suspecting that a principle is at stake, will even oppose such things as free bus rides for parochial-school children. If non-Catholics were really convinced that the major effort of Catholic education was toward greater and greater participation in the public schools, it seems highly likely that aid programs for school children could be enacted which in no way would discriminate against children attending religious schools.

A greater Catholic commitment to public and state schools ought to be realistic, however. All the traditional arguments against state monopoly of education still obtain. The survival of private schools is important, not least for the challenge they can constantly provide for public schools. It is for the democratic genius of the American people to use the State, and not to be used by it. Only articulate and responsible local control of education can help public schools avoid bureaucracy and standardization, and can help them find solutions in terms of community needs.

Are we Catholics completely logical in complaining that the atmosphere of much in public education is unfriendly to religious values when we have systematically withdrawn our own students and the majority of our best minds from the public schools? We have cried out for so long that the schools are godless that perhaps we have at least partially brought our fears into being. Are we to continue our withdrawal?

This would seem the "safer" thing to do (although the rise in costs and the decline in vocations among teaching orders must give us some doubts as to whether it is possible). But these public schools are our schools too. If their secularist bias continues to gain the ascendancy, the experiment in American general education must be deemed a failure, and the loss for the nation at large will be incalculable. Our responsibility, both toward our children and our country, should be to unite with those who are increasingly aware—and many of them are already at work in the public-school system—that this trend should be reversed.

This will not be accomplished by noisy and strenuous "patriot" groups; it has nothing to do with removing Howard Fast's books from public high-school libraries. The basic idea of the American public school is compromised insofar as its training militates against the formation of the *homo naturaliter Christianus*. Catholics, Protestants, Jews, agnostics, and even secularists can work together so that the graduates of the public schools will at least pose to themselves the problem of their destiny. Since the public school cannot undertake doctrinal instruction, the Catholic will always rightly consider such "religious" training incomplete; it is, in fact, pre-religious training which the home and the parish must supplement. The public school can only keep the avenues open: both to the supernatural and to a humanism that considers itself self-sufficient.

As the situation stands today, we are understandably hesitant about accepting greater participation in the public school as an ultimate goal. Perhaps the awareness of our own inadequacies in giving our children the religious training they need is one reason for this. But has not our being able to say, "Our boy is under the good sisters' care; our duty is done," often encouraged parental irresponsibility and religious illiteracy? Are not most of our parishes so busy with the financing and administration of their churches, schools, rectories, and convents that there is little money and less time to make sure that adults are continuing to be educated in their faith?

It seems to me that once we adopt the "missionary" understanding of the parish, as preached by an Abbé Godin or an Abbé Michonneau, we will no longer be content to build huge parish plants—which sometimes become as much a monument to our material success as to the honor of God— as insecure islands in a hostile world. Abbé Michonneau has harsh things to say about a pastoral effort almost entirely given over to children. It sometimes seems to him an evasion, betraying a kind of fear that the Gospel can no longer be preached as relevant to the parents. The priest who cannot speak of poverty in Wall Street, of justice and purity of heart in the factory, of peace and mercy in the training camp, may be grievously deceiving himself when he rejoices to see the parish athletic teams he has organized filling up the first three rows at Mass.

The necessity for more vocations to the priesthood is real, but it is hard to take the problem as seriously as it should be taken when we see so many of those who have received the sacrament of Holy Orders bending most of their energies to all kinds of administrative tasks, teaching chemistry, English, or for that matter, the higher courses in philosophy. If it is claimed that this is necessary, that these priests cannot be free for the full-time discharge of their sacerdotal duties, the answer would seem to be that this is further proof of the uneconomic nature of the Catholic educational effort.

Until recently, lack of trained personnel made the use of

priests necessary in many leading positions in Catholic schools. It is not a complaint against their teaching—probably the majority of the Church's most distinguished scholars are priests even today—to say that the Catholic people who built and maintained a high level of seminary training were hoping for full-time priests, and were not intentionally subsidizing clerical scholarship.

American Catholicism could not have made the gains it has without a close relationship between priests and people. Laymen can teach arithmetic and even theology; they cannot take the place of the priest in a world dying with a thirst for the sacred. Priests who are good bookkeepers or good English teachers are not bearing their uniquely healing word to the people, visiting each apartment in a crowded tenement block, spending the extra afternoon with patients in a mental hospital, making it possible for more souls to have the individual spiritual advisers they need.

The decisions of American Catholics in education will be fateful for the Church and for the nation. Laymen should have sufficient loyalty to their bishops to make their opinions and hopes known, with no reservations about their willingness to co-operate, whatever direction is to be taken. Whatever may be the future of the Catholic school system, I think we have reviewed enough of the situation to come to some conclusions:

(1) The financial burden of parochial schools should not obscure American Catholic responsibility for the support of public education. Catholics should never allow themselves to be the inveterate opposition on increases for public-school budgets, and should do more than they now seem to be doing to earn a reputation as friends of the public school.

(2) New Catholic schools should not be started "automatically." In those that exist a greater effort should be made to avoid whatever logic there may be in this system that might make for an exaggerated separation and any trace of intolerance.

(3) Existing Catholic schools, and indeed the planning of the over-all Catholic educational effort, ought to be more and more in the hands of qualified laymen, leaving more priests free to institute a genuine parish revival looking toward increased religious education for adults and closer contact with the people.

The American experiment has led to the very brink of religious indifferentism, a situation to which Catholics must ever be alert. But we sometimes forget the positive values of this experiment, and need to be reminded of some of them, as in the statement of Dr. Judah Goldin, Dean of Seminary College, Jewish Theological Seminary: "In this country even the non-public schools have been influenced in fundamental ways to the good by the character of our public schools. . . . [They] have done much to ease the unnecessary strains that exist among the various sects and denominations. I think that even the denominational schools, because of the parallel existence of our public schools, have learned how to make their particular emphases with better grace and greater fairness."

Julian Pleasants

CATHOLICS AND
SCIENCE

K IND words about natural science come from eminent
churchmen at regular intervals. Kind words about religion come from eminent scientists with somewhat less regularity, but the deficiency is made up by repeated quotation.
This mutual commendation, unhappily, is of little use in an-
swering the question: What is the *actual* relationship between
American Catholics and natural science as it operates, and
American Catholics as they operate? Is it a happy marriage,
a divorce, or a simple case of nonsupport? To tell the truth,
when Catholics themselves began to get perturbed about it,
fifteen or twenty years ago, it looked like no more than a mild
and tentative flirtation. How are they getting along together
now?

American Catholicism, as it now operates in the area native
to research, maintains about 14 per cent of the institutions of
higher learning in this country, attended by about 10 per cent
of American college students. This educational system is still
in the process of establishing itself. It is heavily unendowed,
and survives by the constant sacrifices of both religious and
laity. Above the college level, it produces a really outstanding number of lawyers, and a quite respectable number of

physicians and businessmen. In producing eminent writers or artists or social theorists, the system is rather less than successful. The production of outstanding natural scientists is something else again than the number of science professors on the faculty or the number of science graduates. Various ways of estimating Catholic effort in scientific research have been used, none entirely satisfactory, but it is remarkable how the various estimates agree.

Catholic schools *are* doing research in natural sciences. That is a point that needs to be made at the outset. The larger Catholic universities, such as Notre Dame, Catholic University, Marquette, and St. Louis, are spending in the neighborhood of a half-million dollars a year apiece on research in the natural sciences, and the extent of their investment is increasing rapidly. This investment is more than many state universities reported to the New York *Times* last year, more than that of many old established colleges, like Amherst or Colgate, not a great deal less than Duke's $850,000 or Stanford's $1,000,000. Needless to say, it falls below Princeton's $2,200,000, or Minnesota's $5,250,000, or Illinois' $7,214,000, or Cornell's $14,850,000. Besides what the larger universities do, some of the smaller Catholic colleges, particularly girls' schools, are making modest but well-planned forays into research, and are qualifying for grants.

In between, however, is set a great void, so that in the aggregate, a decided difference emerges between Catholic and non-Catholic effort in research. The data of A. B. Corrigan in the April 11, 1953, issue of *America* indicated that in 1950 the Catholic colleges, with 12 per cent of the college enrollment, spent 1 per cent of the money spent by colleges on research. Eight dollars was spent on research per Catholic student contrasted with approximately a hundred spent per student in non-Catholic schools. In 1953, with the total research investment of colleges and universities at the $350,000,000 level, Catholic schools' investment might be estimated at about $4,000,000.

This 1 per cent figure also crops up frequently in the reports of agencies that sponsor research. (The bulk of the funds spent on research, even by the colleges, comes from the federal government, industry, and foundations.) The National Science Foundation, set up by Congress to help finance basic research, especially in schools less favored by other government agencies, gives about 1 per cent of its money to Catholic institutions. It would like to give them a more proportionate share, since this is public money and perhaps 20 per cent of it comes from Catholics, directly or indirectly, but the applications do not come in. The same is true of other public funds, such as those of the American Cancer Society, which gave 1 per cent of its funds to Catholic schools in 1951 and ¼ of 1 per cent during the five years preceding. Some other foundations, like the Damon Runyon Fund, are able to place more grants (4 per cent of their total) in Catholic schools, but their fellowship funds go begging for applicants from Catholic schools. (I mention these agencies with a medical slant particularly because American Catholics have made notable contributions to medical care in this country in the way of doctors and hospitals, and it might be expected that they would carry this impulse through into the field of research.)

This rate of participation is, nevertheless, quite a bit higher than the participation in industrially sponsored grants in 1946, when the National Research Council published a listing. Catholic schools reported grants that amounted to ⅕ of 1 per cent of the total, or one dollar in every five hundred.

Other standards of comparison give similar results. In 1951, Professors Knapp and Goodrich published a study purporting to show that the small liberal arts colleges were the mothers of eminent scientists, even if the prospective scientists had to go elsewhere for the advanced studies. The survey incidentally showed that Catholic schools at any level were turning out one-sixth as many eminent scientists, proportionately, as the non-Catholic schools. But twenty years earlier, when Lehmann and Witty published a similar survey with somewhat higher qualifications, the proportion was even less. Out of 1,189 scientists voted eminent by colleagues in their own field, there were at that time only three who listed themselves as Catholic in their biographical sketches. This is one in four hundred, as compared with one in six in 1951.

In 1938, Professors Reyniers and Bauer made a comprehensive survey of Catholics' scientific productivity in terms of published articles. The survey was broadened to include publication in other academic fields. Less than one-fifth of the Catholic scientific writers had published anything original, and comparison with non-Catholic contributions indicated that Catholics had about one-fourth as many faculty members capable of original production as the Catholic population of the country would lead us to expect. The scientific productivity was even less than the general productivity, but the eye-opening discovery was the revelation that Catholics had no special prejudice against scientific research, and yet seemed little interested in original research in any field. Scientific research, being the most expensive, apparently suffered most from a general lack of interest.

Figures being compiled now by Professor Reyniers indicate so far that during the fifteen years from 1938 to 1953, while total college research investment increased fifteen-fold, Catholic investment increased even faster. No one has yet integrated all the available data into a clear picture, but from collaboration with Reyniers and Bauer on analyzing some of their data, I come away with two strong, though not necessarily exact impressions. Twenty years ago, Catholic effort in scientific research was perhaps one-thirtieth of that done by an equal number of non-Catholics. Right now, Catholic effort is probably one-tenth of what would be expected from a comparable group of non-Catholics, despite the fact that a few Catholic centers are developing their resources very rapidly.

Here we have an approximate and strictly comparative idea of what the American Catholic effort in science was and is. What ought it to be? The amount of scientific research done by non-Catholic schools at the moment does not necessarily represent the norm. Many educators who cannot be accused of prejudice against science are still worried at the effect upon general education of the present emphasis on research in natural sciences. The money spent by colleges on such research has increased fifteen-fold in fifteen years, to the point where in some colleges it makes up from 25 to 69 per cent of the total budget. On top of that, most of the money spent comes from the federal government, a new and potentially dangerous situation for institutions jealous of their freedom.

But the difference in scientific accomplishment between Catholics and non-Catholics is still striking, and the simple explanations simply do not explain. The plea of Catholic poverty induced by support of a separate school system has its element of truth, yet there are other expensive educational activities that Catholic schools manage to maintain in good condition, such as law schools and athletic teams. Ours is not an abject but a discriminating poverty; it lays bare our scale of values by indicating what we feel we can do without. Catholic administrators who are now making genuine sacrifices to increase scientific research in their colleges do so, in my opinion, with real courage, because they are not being backed up by the Catholic body as a whole. Even if our colleges could not afford much research, they could still, like the small liberal arts colleges of Knapp and Goodrich's survey, start many students on the road to scientific eminence. They are not doing so.

Another common explanation for a lower rate of Catholic research is that the Catholic is not free to do research. In this view, the hierarchy is afraid of new scientific truths that might endanger the docile acceptance of Catholic doctrine. They therefore close off whole areas of research—closing doors that the uninhibited scientist finds open and inviting.

No Catholic with a memory three centuries long could feel hurt at such a suggestion or deny the validity it once had. But this explanation takes no account of the changes wrought by three centuries. The grounds for conflict between scientific discovery and religious teaching have been almost washed away by the tide of advancing science. First to go down was the absolutism that gave ecclesiastical policy the practical force of dogma. As soon as theologians were forced to admit that the literal interpretation of Bible history was a matter of policy and not a matter of creed, the way was opened for a refinement of scientific thinking that has given us a worthier and less anthropomorphic idea of the Creator.

But the major casualty in the advance of science was science itself, at least as the nineteenth century had understood it: a body of proved conclusions about inexorable laws. The relativity theory and quantum mechanics shattered the naïve assumption that a theory was proved if you could use it to predict something new, for they predicted all that the old theories did plus things the old theories would have predicted wrong. The modern scientist is left only with data of which he is never sure. He values his hypotheses according to the way they predict future occurrences and open up new fields of study, but he does not claim that they are proved or certain. His theories are a matter of working policy rather than a scientific creed, as the physicist J. J. Thomson wrote as early as 1907.

It must be admitted that the more vociferous of the scientists have done their best to keep the public from realizing the tentative character of their theories, but the truth will out. In the meantime, the old battleground between science and religion, the field of pre-history, has become a courtroom in which natural science presents its evidence, which is circumstantial, inferential, and incomplete, while religion presents its own evidence, which is eyewitness testimony from an unimpeachable witness, but unfortunately also incomplete and not very clear, since it was given for a different purpose. It is up to the historian to render a verdict as best he is able to do.

The next casualty in the advance of science may well be the doctrine of salvation-by-science-alone, along with its counterpart, salvation-by-religious-formulas-alone. God knows how much more disillusionment we shall have to go through before the conflict resolves itself—disillusionment with the religious man who knows in a general way what to do but not how to do it, and with the scientist who knows how to do it but not what to do. Against repeated assertions from one camp that mankind will be saved from itself by a return to religion and assertions from the other camp that it will be saved by the universal application of scientific method, the common sense of mankind may yet assert itself to declare that neither one alone, nor both together, give us a complete explanation of the universe or a complete guide to action. Religious principles are too ultimate to settle each individual case for us, and science is not ultimate enough really to settle anything.

This brings us, in my opinion, to the basic reason for the striking difference between American Catholics and American non-Catholics in scientific creativity. When Lehmann and Witty found so few Catholics in the ranks of eminent scientists, they remarked: "The conspicuous dearth of scientists among the Catholics suggests that the tenets of that Church are not consonant with scientific endeavor." This is, of course, an understandable but not at all scientific conclusion from the data, because it runs the risk of a sampling error like that made by the four-year-old Protestant girl who went swimming in the brook with a little Catholic boy, though neither had brought along a bathing suit. "My," she remarked, "Catholics are lots different from Protestants."

The modern American Catholic's philosophy of life is not necessarily the product of Catholic doctrine, even when it is peculiar to Catholics as a group. It could mean that we have succumbed to a peculiarly "Catholic" temptation. The modern American Catholic apparently places a very low value on creative activity. Scientific research is just one of these activities. Literature and art are others. Even in the field of creative social reform, where Christian motivation might be expected to be singularly effective, it is hard to escape the impression that American Catholics were moved into their present positions not by any inner sense of responsibility for inventing new social reforms, but by ulterior motives such as the fear of losing the working classes, or the fear of Communism.

172

Catholics and Science

The philosophy of life that is prevalent though by no means universal among American Catholics is, in my opinion, the key to the scarcity of Catholic creativity. Father Joseph Buckley, S.M., may have put his finger on it in 1940 when he contrasted "The Philosophy of Life of Catholics and the Catholic Philosophy of Life" in the *American Ecclesiastical Review:*

Catholics have indeed been taught that the goal to which their life on earth should lead them is heaven and God. But through a gradual and rather indefinite process of reasoning and impression, they have come to feel and think that this goal is to be attained not so much by the positive substance of their lives—of their actions, thoughts and purposes—as in a negative and accidental fashion, by avoiding certain excesses and performing certain actions on the side, as it were, and in passing. Thus they will tell you that provided they avoid mortal sin in their everyday actions and fulfill certain required formalities, such as attending Mass on Sunday, receiving Holy Communion once a year, abstaining from flesh meat on Friday, they will get to heaven.

This prevailing philosophy of life of Catholics is almost sheer formalism, obedience to certain arbitrary prescriptions for the sake of an arbitrary reward. In such a view, salvation is simply an application of definite formulas to a few definite occasions in life. Where the formulas do not apply, the matter is of no real significance. Nothing new need be added. Formalism does not forbid creative activity—it just takes the heart out of it.

Formalism provides no status for the virtues of science, art, and prudence, since they are meaningless to someone who already has all the answers. The idea of Christian life as charity working with the tools of science, art, and prudence to redeem the world becomes equally meaningless. Formalism is the peculiar temptation to which the American Catholic has for the moment succumbed. Lance Wright, in "The Apostolic Role of the University Graduate" (*Downside Review,* Winter 1953), has stated the matter quite succinctly:

> Because the Truths of our religion are handed down to us by tradition, therefore this mode of receiving knowledge is become instinctive in us, and other modes instinctively suspect. . . . This dependence of ours on Tradition for truths of the supernatural order tends to breed in us a form of intellectual sloth which is peculiar to ourselves. Because the Truths which really matter were given once and for all, therefore (we argue) they are in themselves immutable and no subsequent knowledge can touch them in any way: therefore a gulf is fixed between Religious Truth (with a big "T") and secular truth (with a little "t"): therefore the Catholic is absolved from any real intellectual curiosity concerning the things of this world. . . .
>
> This awareness of what is going on in secular knowledge which is so necessary to keep Theology herself alive, is necessary equally if the Truths of Revelation are to be accurately applied to the conduct of everyday life. This seems so obvious. Yet the force of it does not seem to strike the majority of Catholics. What I would myself describe as a strong "clerical" bias seems to make us regard secular knowledge as something lying outside the scheme of Redemption: a sort of hobby for the human race, and nothing to do with the real business of existence.

Traditionalism alone, however, cannot account for the Catholic's intellectual sloth. The Catholic is not *ipso facto* opposed to change. In everyday life he does not stand out conspicuously by his devotion to the customs of the past. He is likely to follow, often uncritically and even slavishly, the prevailing fashions in dress, education, or recreation, though always a little late because he wants to make sure that that is the way things are going. He is willing to use the latest antibiotic, and is glad somebody took the trouble to find it. Yet he does almost nothing to help find a new antibiotic. It is not worth *his* trouble. Despite clannishness in some respects, American Catholics have not tried to swim ashore from the world which science is propelling so rapidly through a series of revolutionary changes. We even seem to be enjoying the ride. But we do not pull an oar. That is the crux of the matter.

In my opinion, the basic difference between this modern world that values research so much, and the Catholic segment that values it so little, is that the Catholic part had given up the virtue of prudence, and the modern world, through the advance of science, rediscovered it. The temptation to give up prudence for formalism is an ever-present temptation for Catholics, since we have it on the highest authority that "the children of the world are more prudent in their generation than the children of light," especially in regard to the things of this world.

The scientific method could not have come upon the world as a new dawn if the sun of prudence had not already set. The modern scientific method is nothing more than the first five steps in prudent judgment. In fact, Saint Thomas Aquinas's exposition of these steps reads like some Science Department's outline for the writing of a thesis: history of the question, present understanding of the question, assembling of the data by search of the literature and by experimental discovery of new data, speculation about the relationships involved (Saint Thomas calls it *eustochia*—happy conjecturing—a most felicitous term), and reasoning from the known to the unknown.

This very prudence, which seems today the property and even the discovery of the scientist, is by right the central governing virtue of Christian life. To it belongs, by right, the spirit of critical investigation, of discovery, invention, and experimentation, whether our aim at the time is to know something, to make something, or to do something.

The modern world may have gone hog wild in making purely natural science, even purely physical science, the basis of its prudence. The scientist and his followers who dash into action armed with the latest laboratory report ("scientific tests show") are more basically imprudent than the members of certain Catholic Action groups who dash into action armed with a survey of the existing situation and a copy of the New Testament. I am not going to argue about that. But that does not alter the fact that the chief aspects of modern science, the spirit of critical inquiry, the spirit of discovery, and the creative spirit from which the grand speculative theories of modern science have been born, are the features most glaringly lacking in modern Catholic life.

The normal proportion of scientific research that we decide upon will reflect very largely our philosophy of life and of education. There are at least two possible Catholic approaches to scientific research, stemming from two different philosophies.

On the one hand, a Catholic may believe that Divine Revelation has provided him with all that he ever needs to know, either to love God worthily or to serve Him well. When he comes to matters about which Revelation has nothing clear to say, then the matter is of no real significance and we can act as we please, or according to the prevailing fashion. Education then consists in handing down the Revelation intact, plus whatever knowledge the student would like to have. Under such conditions, scientific research is at best a luxury that we can ill afford until we have taken care of the necessities, in this case, the necessity of giving a college-level presentation of Revealed Doctrine to as many Catholics as want to go to college for one reason or another.

Another standard for Catholic life and education is the

revelation of God, not only Revelation with a capital "R" but revelation with a small "r": the revelation of the Artist which we find in His art, the revelation of the Lawmaker which we find in His laws, the revelation of the Planner's intentions which we find in the way He has made things. A Catholic college, to reach this standard, must be not only an institution of higher teaching, but an institution of higher learning, a community of people seeking truth, not only passing it from hand to hand. Besides the virtue of obedience, it must logically develop the virtues of science, art, and prudence. Besides the docile acceptance of Divine Revelation, it must develop the requisite attitude toward all that body of human knowledge that is in a state of development. The attitude demanded is neither cynical reserve nor uncritical acceptance, but a spirit of critical inquiry, experimentation, and discovery.

It is easy enough to see how scientific research would fare under one or the other regime. What is not so easy is to see which is the truer picture of the Christian's vocation in the world. I will not presume to argue the theology of the situation, but this much is certain as a matter of observation: science has had, for better and for worse, a tremendous influence upon both religious thought and religious life.

Scientific theories have changed profoundly our notion of the creating of the world, and thereby our notion of and even attitude toward the Creator. Catholic exegesis has found in them a means of refining our literal and anthropomorphic concepts of the Creator. Antireligious forces have exploited them as all-sufficing explanations of a universe that had no Creator. Scientific theories and achievements have enormously widened the scope of human power, freedom, and responsibility, in the control of nature. In the face of disease and malnutrition the medieval Christian practiced the virtue of resignation; the scientist practices the virtue of research (prudence). Much of what we once blamed on God we now blame on ourselves. In fact, we can get so carried away by the successes of human providence as to feel that Divine Providence is only an outmoded hypothesis. Yet the growth in efficiency of human providence has made possible a most Christian determination to wipe out the hunger and disease all over the world that have stood as a living indictment of Christian apathy. While theoretical science has been broadening man's freedom and responsibility, applied science has been building a social structure that seems to take it away again. The mass civilization in which we live has had a profound effect upon religious life and practice, largely by weakening the family as an instrument of education and replacing its influence with mass media of communication.

The list is too long and the weighing too delicate for anyone to render an accounting of the good and evil that have come from scientific research. In the face of what evolutionism and scientism have so obviously done to the religious attitude of so many men, it may take strong faith on the part of Catholic college administrators to believe that the discovery of new truth and the elaboration of new theories is more likely than not to help us know God better and serve Him more prudently. We have to be convinced on a priori grounds that God has made things well, that the more we understand of what He has made, the better we can know Him, and that the more we understand the natures of things, the better we can use them for the purposes for which He made them. Yet nothing in science itself forces us to direct either our thoughts or our actions to God. We have to be ready to run the risk of misdirected science if we are to have science at all.

Catholics and Science

Catholicism and science were meant for each other. In the Church we find the feminine element of life in its perfection. Well is she called "Mother" Church, she who hands down Christian tradition from generation to generation and trains the little ones. Yet the Church as a human institution suffers the temptations of its state, *les défauts de ses qualités:* the temptation to timidity, the temptation to rank custom above life and obedience above prudence. Modern science is a masculine element, inquisitive, daring, critical, willing to try the new, yet careless of holding fast to what is good in the old, lacking often in reverence for human nature and even for things themselves, feeling strangely dissatisfied in the very midst of its triumphs. Each needs the other. Both are suffering from this overlong courtship. The world itself needs their fruitful union. Pope Pius XII, judging by his encouragement of scientific research, stands ready to bless that union. Will it come?

Henry Rago

CATHOLICS AND
LITERATURE

I TAKE it that we are talking about literature in an unqualified sense: simply literature, trying to be as good as it can possibly be. And so, first of all, we have to be clear that such literature would have the same struggle with American Catholics that it has with Americans generally.

The market still belongs to the clever approximation: the processed rather than the genuine. Not that there are no inroads. The national culture is something that history has never seen before, a thing of forced growth, developing under extraordinary pressures. Out of this surely comes all the vulgarity that the reformers have an easy time ridiculing, but at the same time the phenomenon of the paperback classic sold in the hundreds of thousands for thirty-five cents. And first-rate fiction (along with third-rate of course) appears more and more often in the family magazine; and I am not thinking merely of *The New Yorker*. Perhaps it appears *more* often in such magazines than it does in the more specialized literary journals, where, for good reason, the experiment is usually more interesting than the achievement.

Let me not say any more than I mean to say. A fine piece of work can be given a great market while its deepest excellences continue to go unnoticed. What gets the praise may be the high finish; what gets permission in the first place may be the subject matter and the décor. Much remains unpraised; much remains impermissible. We have to say, too, that the recognition goes to the already recognized: to the writer who has already won his battle, or to the kind of treatment that at last has become familiar. Often the scores of imitators, diluting the genuine article with just the right mixture, are well-fed precursors for the real precursor. The good writer who is new—genuinely new—to the public is still difficult, and every time he comes along, in this person or that, he will be difficult. Even at the universities, in America or elsewhere, the new in literature will have to struggle for understanding or even for a reading.

As for the new in poetry, the less said the better. There is no need for anyone to be ill-tempered about this. Poetry, new or old, is strenuous reading. One is pleased and perhaps even a little surprised to come upon people who do read it. One is pleased to find even a novelist who reads it, or a scholar; even a scholar in English literature, if it is new poetry that he is reading. I mean if it is poetry that has not been explained. It is nobody's *business* to read it; not even the English scholar's. Naturally I would like a lot of people to read it— for their sake and for the sake of my fellow poets. And I think that a few more people would enjoy reading it if they tried. But because poetry, at the most typical, is always making an idiom where hitherto there was no idiom, I know what the difficulties are; and I do not think that the Good Society depends on everybody's reading poetry.

For literature from its more popular to its less popular forms, the situation then is one of general resistance, with such progress as we can hopefully and perhaps too eagerly detect. In all this the American Catholic will share as he shares in American culture generally. Up to this point we see him only as part of the statistics in the common problem of the "general reader" in America.

It is here that we can begin to see the peculiar complication he brings to this problem. I would say that it is a three-fold complication, and I see it best in terms of two vices and one virtue.

One vice might well be called the Double Standard. There is literature and then, *miserere*, there is "Catholic" literature. Literature has to be good; Catholic literature has to be "Catholic." It is as if one read each of these literatures with a separate sensibility; or, where "Catholic" literature is concerned, with *in*sensibility. In its best practice, this tendency causes even a good Catholic writer to be praised in grotesque disproportion to his true merit, and at the same time it denies him the professional standards, which, as a matter of both pride and honesty, he would want to be measured by. In its worst practice this vice would lead one to think that the sacrament of baptism, even when received fairly late in life, forgave not only mortal and venial sins but also faults of style.

How stubborn this habit of judgment is, I do not have to tell the conscientious teacher in the Catholic universities or the conscientious critic in the few literate Catholic magazines. They and their small audience find themselves in the ungrateful role of dissenters, scolds, or prophets of culture, constantly having to repeat what is as boring for them as it is annoying to others, all in the simple business of trying to be honest.

I have put it this way—in terms of honesty—because I do not think that any movement needs to be started, any battle fought, or any reform made in the name of culture. I am not urging the importance of esthetic values; I am only urging

183

honesty in judging them when one sets about judging them at all. There is no question of a choice between art and piety—the choice for a Christian is quite clearly decided—although I do not think that the choice arises, in authentic terms, as frequently as we are led to think when we read "Catholic" criticism. Even when the choice is made, we should be doubly careful not to confuse piety with art by praising the vulgar for the sake of piety but in the name of art: that is no choice at all but an attempt to have it both ways.

Ideally the choice need not be made. Piety is free of the demands of art not by cheating those demands but by transcending them. Surely there are the special purposes of devotional reading; and those purposes are quite apart from and quite superior to esthetic pleasure. But if the purpose is high, so much the greater insult to it if the writer or the reader cheats to attain it. Saint Augustine does not cheat. Saint John of the Cross does not cheat. Distortion, exaggeration, sentimentality, these are distractions from contemplation, not helps to it. In them a man only flatters himself or does something far worse, for I think there is a sense in which one can speak of flattering God. Flattery is not praise but the *use* of praise. These are contraries: for praise gives, and flattery solicits; praise rejoices in truth, and flattery makes its own truth; praise comes from faith, flattery from the lack of it.

In the light of this the Double Standard begins to show itself as Multiple. There is the tendency to divide literature into two parts, the shabbier part being "Catholic," and within that section to divide it again in order to get a separate esthetic standard—or no esthetic standard at all—for devotional reading. Even further divisions might be possible and in fact are implicitly made, for the notion of a Catholic literature is at best ambiguous.

Catholics and Literature

Is it literature *by* Catholics? On any subject at all, including some of the obiter dicta I have seen appearing in the same advertisement with patristics and hagiography? Apparently some special standard canonizes even the most casual scribblings of the Guaranteed Catholic Author. Is it literature *for* Catholics but not necessarily *by* Catholics? I think I have seen such literature given even more special treatment, usually in some form whereby the reader manages to congratulate both the author and himself. The Holy Spirit breathes where It will, but there is an ever vigilant cheering section capable of following these manifestations and even attempting to direct them. The Scripture tells us to rejoice for the lost sheep brought home; but when the cheers express a wish for the slick triumph in argument, the hit with the newspapers, the proprietorship over the truth rather than the humble living in the faith of it, I rather suspect that what we have is not a lost sheep but a golden calf.

Or is Catholic literature (if one must use the term at all) any work in which there is some implication of the Christian concept of man? If this is so, we can leave our discussion of the Double Standard, now Multiple, and turn to the second vice, not unrelated to it. Let us call it Xenophobia.

Literature is many countries and many ages and many beliefs, clear or clouded. It has its own legitimacy and its own goodness; it is its own world and an extraordinary one, for merely to enter is to be enfranchised. It asks us to make no excuses for our coming to it, except the wonder and delight it promises. The entrance can be made only in the same spirit. Its full skies and its full landscape will not open to those who do not *wish* to enter; or to those who enter without the wish—I mean to say, by force. Those who would take it over in the name of politics, or psychology, or anthropology, or even religion are using force. Oddly enough, they will not even get what they are looking for.

Religious values, in their full depth and complexity, cannot be wrenched from literature without some feeling for the art and some sense of its tradition in the full scope. The point (again) is not whether literature is important or unimportant; if anything, I would argue that literature is relatively unimportant. This is a way of saying that it is not religion nor even the confirmation of religion.

The point here is the tendency among American Catholics, and not only the uninstructed, to refuse the exploration of literature on these terms. I leave it to others to discuss the basic sociology of which this is only one manifestation. The tendency as it concerns us here is puritanical, negativistic, defensive, and rather nervous. Obviously, these characteristics go a long way toward explaining the Double Standard as well as Xenophobia. And I can wonder sometimes whether they are the result of one's having faith or the result of one's *not* having quite as much faith as one would like to think one has.

Recently a colleague at the university where I teach told me that he had met one of my friends, a priest, at a meeting of a philosophical association. My colleague was greatly impressed to meet a priest so thoroughly inside the problems of contemporary philosophy and so open to their consideration in the terms they demand. I understood my colleague's surprise, but in my own feelings there was no surprise at all. A man of genuine faith and genuine charity does not need cheap assurances, nor does he need to strain for intellectual generosity. Such a man is free, and the center of his freedom is not a philosophy; it is not even a theology; it is faith, which is infinitely beyond both. Paradoxically this faith can make philosophy most truly itself: the love of wisdom. Love is the opposite of fear.

As with philosophy, so, surely, with literature. Although literature has its own subtle relations to truth, its claims on truth are more humble than those of philosophy. If philosophy begins with wonder, literature is content to end where philosophy begins; for literature asks us not to judge a possibility but only to delight in it, not to believe but to wonder.

I mention the "subtle relations to truth" without analyzing them; they would require a complete disquisition on a problem that has exercised most of the critics of our time. I give the problem no treatment rather than an unjust and distorted simplification. It is enough to say here that "truth" does not guarantee literary merit, nor does literary merit guarantee "truth." I am afraid that literature simply has to be read before it can be judged, even before it can be judged for "truth."

I intended, after talking about two vices, to talk of one virtue. That virtue should now be obvious; we have been assuming it all through this discussion, and it has been making itself clearer and clearer as the center of the entire problem. The virtue is Christian faith. We have already seen it in its distortions. But we have been seeing also that in its purity it is the very poise and the very freedom of the free mind. It comes to literature, as it comes to everything, with complete largesse; it can afford literature as it can afford everything; it is the acceptance of all that is.

The Christian will find deeper reason than Terence had for saying that nothing human is alien to him. By the central mystery of the Incarnation, he has commitments everywhere and in everything; he will refuse nothing, as the Logos, which is his life, refuses no history. If he suffers amid the divisions of the secular movements of his time, it is in the division itself that his suffering is most profound; it is in what these movements *refuse*. He will not bargain with literature or with anything else in the world to give him what only his faith can give him completely, and he will love literature more, for loving it freely.

This is the ideal. In the incomparably humble problem of reading literature, it manifests itself where it manifests itself. For most of us, it is best described as a virtuality rather than as a virtue. One mentions it not as a fact of history but as a hope.

Meanwhile, by and large, the hope is not lived up to. The best critics in America are, most of them, not Catholic. The most pure-minded reading of literature is done, generally speaking, at the non-Catholic universities. And the best way to see so nebulous a matter as the place of the Catholic among the more literate "general readers" is to reflect that the serious Catholic writer in America writes "for" an audience that is chiefly non-Catholic. I am not adept at statistics but even in these broad statements I am trying to take into account the fact that Catholics are a minority in this country.

Nor can I soften these remarks by agreement with those who speak of a Catholic literary revival. I do not think it exists in America. We can say that there is a handful of good writers who are Catholics, only a handful, and since we are concerned with reading rather than writing, the most we can say is that the best of them refuse an easy reading, so that in reading them at all the Catholic must become aware of literary values in their own right. This may be a circumstance that was not present in the typical Catholic predilections of, say, twenty or thirty years ago. The circumstance is reinforced by the demands which a handful of English and French Catholic writers also make on their readers. But this is a circumstance, not necessarily a sign of anything greater to come; and even as a circumstance it has only to be placed in the long history of literature to indicate an epoch somewhat less than luminous. The French contribution would seem greatest. But I would say that the "revival" in France is much more intellectual than artistic. Among the creative writers I see only one artist of the magnitude of Valéry, Proust, and Gide; that is Paul Claudel.

But it should be clear that the question of a Catholic literary revival is largely irrelevant, except as it would induce more Catholics to read. The dangers of so special an inducement also ought to be clear. (I cannot help noticing that the inducement itself is somewhat questionable, even on its own grounds: if it is a question of reading literature for a Christian view of life, I would spend very little time with some of the writers who are frequently mentioned in connection with a Catholic literary revival, and I would find much more completeness and compassion in the work of writers who happen not to be Catholic.)

The inducement to literature should be literature. The *interference* with it can be left to the rationalists, the short-term optimists, the partisans of political slogans, and the "sociopsychological" critics impetuous to decide what is "healthy" and what is "unhealthy." All these have been active in their operations on modern literature. Each is a dogmatist not because he has a dogma he believes but because he has a dogma he wishes to *institutionalize,* and he would like to take literature over for the purpose. But literature is not to be possessed;

it is to be enjoyed. In the Epilogue to *The Tempest* it is the pure delight of the audience—the applause of their "good hands"—that sets Prospero free and enables the play to be complete. Here wisdom defers to joy, and perhaps this pure joy is its own kind of wisdom.

Dan Herr

READING AND WRITING

ALTHOUGH it is the fashion these days among status-viewers to take a definitely gloomy view of the present position of American Catholics, I must confess that the reading situation among Catholics seems to me much brighter than most of us had hoped for even ten years ago. I mean, of course, that more and more Catholics have discovered—well, let's say the shameful words and be done with it—Catholic books.

For many years now Catholic writers, critics, and teachers have been engaged in an ivory-tower revival meeting featuring shrill debate over what might be loosely described as art for art's sake *versus* art for salvation's sake, changing pace from time to time by locking jaws over the terms "Catholic writer" and "Catholic book." Meanwhile an increasing number of Catholic laymen, ignorant of this death struggle, have quietly exhibited a rather marked interest in Catholic reading—unaware that there is no such thing, or if there is there should not be.

I might as well admit right now that I have little sympathy with all this nose-looking-down, back-bending, and soul-searching about Catholic books prevalent today. To listen to some Catholics you would think it a social error that we admit such categories as Catholic books and Catholic writers. Granting the need to fight any further trend toward separatism or the so-called "ghetto complex," granting that we still suffer from the seemingly inevitable consequences of a minority status, granting that too many Catholics prefer to withdraw from the main stream of American life, I maintain it is downright silly not to recognize that books written from a Catholic theological point of view can be called Catholic books without demanding or disgracing anyone and that a Catholic who writes is a Catholic writer and not, as some haughtily insist, a writer who happens to be a Catholic. An intelligent adult just doesn't *happen* to be a Catholic—or if he does he should be ashamed to admit it—and a writer cannot help but be influenced by the most important fact in his existence: his Catholic faith.

It was not too long ago that most Catholic readers, although recognizing that such a thing as Catholic books existed, thought of them as badly written, pious tracts intended for scrupulous old ladies. The heartening increase in Catholic reading has come from the discovery that such is not the case.

Many factors are responsible, including more writers, better books, and better publishing and merchandising, but the outstanding single factor, I think, was Thomas Merton's *The Seven Storey Mountain*. (If it had not been this book it would have been another, for the time had come.) Catholics who ordinarily would not be caught awake with a Catholic book read Father Merton's autobiography because it was a best seller that was being talked about. Many were shocked to find that here was a Catholic book that called for no apology—it was a good book by any standard. Intrigued by the possibility of other well-written, nonpietistic Catholic books, they investigated further and found them. The word began to spread and before long we had a small-time boom, a boom which fortunately gives the appearance of being with us for a while and possibly even continuing to grow. If any evidence is needed that Catholic books no longer can be dismissed as collections of devotional pamphlets, the current spectacle of general publishers jumping through transoms in an attempt to obtain manuscripts from Catholic writers should be rather convincing.

Lest this growing audience of Catholic readers give cause for unrestrained enthusiasm, I would like to point out that it remains relatively small compared to the millions of Catholics in America. Like most non-Catholic Americans, most Catholics do not read at all unless it be what publisher Frank Sheed has called "spitting-over-the-bridge reading," reading to pass the time or to keep from thinking. Even among those who do read, the majority are interested only in the best seller, and in their reading habits, at least, cannot be distinguished from those of their non-Catholic neighbors. (Some would argue this is all to the good. I disagree.)

I suggest, too, that we may have overestimated the influence of Catholic books on our fellow Americans. Except for a rarity like *The Seven Storey Mountain* and the output of a few writers like Graham Greene, Evelyn Waugh, and Bruce Marshall, Catholic books have yet to reach the regular reading audience. The increased literary tempo in the Catholic field is, I suspect, unknown to most non-Catholic critics and readers. Many publishers, as I have said, are aware of it, but that is only because the bells on their cash registers keep ringing. The job of making Catholic books a vital force in American life remains to be accomplished.

A far greater worry at the moment, however, is the need for Catholic writers. We face the danger that, if our reading audience keeps growing, it may soon outdistance the writers and we will be treated to the unhappy spectacle of readers all ready to read and finding a fairly bare literary cupboard.

We continue to be distressingly dependent on foreign writers for the best of our Catholic literary fare. If the next version of the McCarran Act prohibits the importation of foreign writings, we would lose François Mauriac, Giovanni Guareschi, Evelyn Waugh, Reginald Garrigou-Lagrange, Sheila Kaye-Smith, Gerald Vann, Ronald Knox, Bruce Marshall, C. C. Martindale, Antonin Sertillanges, Daniel-Rops, Karl Stern, Georges Bernanos, and many, many more who are usually considered among our best. As a matter of fact, we would have far too little left, and in the field of fiction we would be paupers. More and more publishers are scanning foreign catalogues for new Catholic books and new writers, and it is no longer a secret that the more successful are the ones who do the fastest scanning, or, better still, regularly hunt and trap in Europe in person. But when you are told that new young writers do not seem to be bursting forth in Europe, either, and that it is by no means certain the balding old stand-bys will have replacements when they have done their bit, you find real reason for concern.

I wish I could present a snap solution to this problem because I believe it should have a priority among the many that face American Catholics today. We desperately need more and better Catholic writers and yet the prospects are not sufficient to encourage any but the most optimistic. It is small comfort to realize that American Catholics share the need for new writers with the rest of Americans—new faces are needed in every phase of American writing.

It seems to me that a small finger could be pointed at Catholic schools and colleges for contributing to this drought. Whatever the reason, they are not turning out enough Catholic readers, much less Catholic writers. Possibly, the latter is not the job of schools, but I think it is. In some cases the schools do not seem to recognize the importance of creating conditions conducive to drawing out young talent. In others, teachers apparently are more interested in strait-jacketing or molding their students to conform than in developing individuality. The most unfortunate error, however, is overselling zeal and forgetting to stress the necessity for competence and hard work. Too many young Catholic writers have been told so often how easy it is to change the world that they are horrified to discover it is not only not easy but takes a terrific amount of sweat even to make a dent. Apostolic zeal is to be desired, but it is not a substitute for hard work. The sooner young Catholic writers learn this—and the best place to learn it is in school—the better for writers, publishers, and readers.

The Catholic press figures prominently in this whole problem. Our magazines and newspapers proclaim how dependent they are on a handful of wheel horses who seem to be working night and day to give the readers something—anything. More important, however, the Catholic press offers a barren field for those who might be interested in serving their writing apprenticeship while serving the cause of Catholic writing. Far too many are edited and almost completely staffed by priests—only about a half-dozen Catholic magazines in America are in the hands of laymen. And even among those that do have room for laymen, the financial aspect of the jobs is sometimes the least appealing. Writers who wish to sell to Catholic magazines will find, with a few notable exceptions, that writing for the love of it is no idle jest.

Critics and reviewers, too, I think, must share part of the blame, particularly those who insist on overpraising anything Catholic, to the extent that our writers are deprived of the occasional kicking around they deserve and would benefit from. For example, it is rare to see an objective review of a convert autobiography. Far too often the review is devoted to welcoming the convert and praising him—left unsaid may be the obvious truth that he writes like a high-school sophomore. This tendency is even stronger in reviews of spiritual writing. Many reviewers apparently do not agree with Thomas Merton that bad writing is bad writing even though it be about the love of God. (There is the other extreme, of course, that affects a hypercritical approach to any Catholic book. As yet this point of view has relatively few adherents, but even so, it seems to me the lesser evil.) Both writers and publishers are frequently getting by with the mediocre and the shoddy because too much of what passes as book reviewing in the Catholic press does not nail down bad writing. Even charity, if that is what it is, can be carried too far.

Earlier I mentioned the by now old-hat but still durable controversies among some writers and critics as to the nature of Catholic literature, its desirability and purpose. Such discussions if kept in perspective are, of course, of interest and of value. Possibly these questions and similar ones must be settled in our day, but I see a growing danger in too many young Catholic writers and some of their not-too-young brethren so occupying themselves with these supersonic arguments that confusion and uncertainty result. This state of mind has helped neither the output nor the quality of modern Catholic writing. Maybe it is time to urge on these theorists the advice of Sinclair Lewis to an audience of young hopefuls: If you want to be writers, why aren't you home writing?

As is true in other spheres of American life, this confusion and uncertainty seem to be increasingly characteristic of the American Catholic approach to literature. A small but growing segment of intellectual Catholics who feel cut off from the main body of the Church in America are reflected in, and act as an influence on, Catholic writing. More and more this rather fluid group seems to draw in upon itself and away from the majority; except for the faith they hold in common they seem to have little respect and even less sympathy for their fellow religionists. As for the majority, they scarcely know the others exist, or, if they do, they think of them as a weird collection of fanatics.

This situation invites the twin perils of snobbism and self-pity. We can foresee this group accepting with a great show of resignation the failure of the uninitiated to appreciate them or even give them a hearing. Reasonably enough, they may find it easier to write primarily for those who will accept and applaud them, and thus may grow among American Catholics the concept of the chosen few who in despair have given up for lost the rest of the world and are content to write for and to influence each other.

Any further move in this direction will put an essential part of Catholic literature about two notches above much of modern poetry. If many of our Catholic writers lose touch with the great body of Catholic readers, consciously or unconsciously look down upon them and feel more kinship with similar esoteric non-Catholic groups, the Church will have suffered a great loss.

I do not wish to suggest that a policy of sacrificing principles, artistic or otherwise, or of consciously writing down to the "underprivileged" is in order. But can we not ask for as much tolerance for differences of opinions among Catholics as most of these same people would rightly demand for differences among races? The application of a live-and-let-live philosophy and an effort by some of our intellectuals to know and understand better the great body of American Catholics, lay and clerical, would, I believe, be of inestimable value to the Church in America. I am not maintaining that the majority is always right and the few are wrong—I am simply hoping that we do not widen the chasm that seemingly already exists between many Catholic artists and the majority of American Catholics.

There is always with us the so-called pious novel, seldom if ever deserving to be classed as literature no matter how general the definition, and in too many cases distressingly inept by any reasonable standards. Yet these novels have filled a need and there are still many who read them for inspiration and entertainment. This audience cannot be ignored nor does it seem fair to attempt to deprive it of what it finds helpful unless the deprivers are prepared to promote a wider appreciation for better writing and make such writing available on a popular level. We have on the one hand a body of current writing worthy of the increasing audience that it attracts and then we have "popular" Catholic writing, until now usually associated with the hack and the amateur. We will always need more writing aimed at the Catholic intellectual but I know of no good reason why the quality of popular writing cannot be improved. The possible good to be achieved is surely worth the effort.

Just as certain techniques or gimmicks are almost always found in the pious novel, so does more advanced Catholic writing tend to be characterized by certain peculiarities. Realism, even if unnecessarily dragged in, seems to be one of these, and realism for realism's sake may soon become the trademark of the better Catholic novel. The pious novel has almost always canonized priest characters. Almost hysterical enthusiasm, therefore, greeted writers who began to show that priests were human beings, too. But as the fashion continues and the human side of the priesthood more and more obscures the divine, the neurotic misfit priest becomes just as much of a type and just as unreal as his sanctimonious counterpart in the pious novel. Now that the novelty and the shock of seeing priests presented as alive and breathing have passed by, it might be time to jump off the new treadmill.

Perhaps this rigidity may come from an effort to depart as far as possible from the traditional American Catholic writing, much of which certainly invited a quick change of pace and direction. Many of the old shibboleths have now been discarded, however, and little is to be gained from a continued conscious reaction against the past. Being different just for the sake of being different will produce no masterpiece.

How and if the problems that confront all those interested in the future of Catholic writing and reading in America—and there are more problems than I have indicated—will be worked out is difficult to forecast. The future seems to be more hopeful than others will admit and certainly it would be a mistake to infer from the emphasis given the darker side that I minimize the progress made, or the possibility of even greater accomplishments. I hope that we will see the day when all American Catholics will be as concerned with promoting the best in reading as they are in damning the worst.

Maurice Lavanoux

CATHOLICS AND
RELIGIOUS ART

I
N THE present temper of life in these United States, art is
still widely looked upon as a mere luxury without any real
relevance. A superficial acceptance of art in general, shared
by many who may hesitate to admit their real indifference,
results in the lack of what may be termed an artistic climate
in which art would be accepted as a normal activity of any
civilized community rather than as something that stamps the
artist as a rather curious and impractical person, to be encouraged, of course, but not to be elevated to the status of a serious
citizen.

Fortunately, our troubles in this respect are of recent date,
and there is growing evidence that art will someday come into
its own in America. In the early days of this country's existence
the need to wrest a living from the land did not leave much
time for the pursuit of art. Later, when the goods of this world
increased in America, and the age of great fortunes came, art
in Europe was in the throes of Victorianism. It was an era in
which those who controlled the nation's purse strings developed a curious inferiority complex and felt drawn toward
Europe for the satisfaction of their artistic needs. It was the
era of the snob in art; an era during which the arbiters of

"taste" felt the urge to add a little polish to their democratic escutcheons through vicarious association with some vague idea of an older tradition. This tradition, because of a basic misunderstanding, had become a static frame of mind instead of what tradition, per se, really is—dynamic.

During this period French châteaux and Florentine palaces were built all over prosperous America. It was then, too, that ecclesiastical art sought refuge and escape in the unfolding arms of archeology. The châteaux and palaces have gradually disappeared, but we still have with us relics of archeology in the arts of the Church. And these relics still increase and multiply.

The present state of religious art among American Catholics, and particularly among the clergy, is sad. It seems to me that it stems largely from indifference and a calculated misuse of the virtue of prudence, which might more properly be called timidity. In addition to this indifference there is a tendency, among our clergy, to equate excellence in artistic matters with the personal piety and goodness of an artist. I will not indulge in the facile sport of placing all the blame on the shoulders of the clergy, but, with all due respect, I can express the opinion that much of the continued patronage of mediocre sources of supply comes from those whose vocation should lead them to sponsor artists who can create the beauty that should be found in the house of God. Too many of our churches reflect mediocrity. Those who have labored in the firms from which emerge creations of dubious "archeology" can do little but weep—or perhaps laugh at the memory of it all! But it is not enough to weep when we see what are called the arts of church decoration, and all the appurtenances used in our churches. We still have enough indignation left to gnash our teeth in anger against the benevolent indifference under which such a disease has been allowed to spread so widely.

Here a sense of humor is useful. Without the saving grace of laughter, and a modicum of ridicule, those who have at heart the propagation of beauty would become bitter indeed. Stout heart and strong optimism are both needed antidotes.

Art is really an important matter in the life of a Catholic and more particularly the arts at the service of the Church. I realize that a Catholic can save his soul without any particular manifestation of art in his daily life, even in his religious life, but if we follow such a point of view to its logical—or illogical—conclusion, we might say that a Catholic can save his soul without a church *building* or without any of those things that have been created for the glory of God and as an earthly expression of the love of God. All we really need is an altar and a tent to cover the congregation—and, at times, we can even do without the tent. But once we admit the advisability of a *house* and all that goes with it, we admit the necessity to have the *best*. And here we come into the province of art. So the question of religious art really is important.

Where can we turn for positive direction in this matter of religious art? Will the dominant factor come from the hierarchy, the pastors, the seminary professors? It should come from all these, but more particularly it should come from the architect. He is the director of that symphony that brings unity and order; he is the one who should logically co-ordinate all the elements that go to make up a beautiful church, inside and out. If we seek direction from the seminaries, we will be faced at once with the lack of any truly artistic direction in the curriculum or with the statement that such training cannot find a place in the already overcrowded course of studies. If we seek direction from the hierarchy we find it already exists in pronouncements from Rome, whether in such documents as *Mediator Dei* or in recent texts from the Holy Office. However, these pronouncements deal in generalities and do not attempt to solve day-to-day problems.

I feel we will find the key to many of these vexing problems when we can convince the pastor that good art, great art, can and does bring to his people that important stimulus of beauty which we all naturally feel to be the proper attribute of the house of God. I feel we will reach that desired goal when we realize that both the pastor and his bishop do not—or, at any rate, should not—claim infallibility in matters of art. In such matters they are persons like ourselves, with personal prejudices and limitations. It is only natural that they should seek guidance from those who are trained in the arts and crafts. It has been my experience that many a bishop or pastor will respond once he is convinced of the validity of an art adviser's or architect's ideas.

There is hope. In recent years good work has been accomplished, and the "archeologists," today, are on the defensive. A defensive, however, whose last stimulus has come from the controversy over that convenient bugaboo, "modern art." This bugaboo is the twin of the distrust and fear engendered by those for whom the mere hint of a fresh idea is cause for alarm. And yet a fresh idea may well be in the grand tradition of the old. It may be, of course, that the accelerated tempo of our day has confused us, and we may yearn for a more peaceful sequence of events, but to yearn for the past is a futile sport. The architect of our time is faced with certain economic facts that did not bother architects of old; we have certain changes in the plans of our churches that are quite logical in the light of liturgical observance. There is no mystery in all this and no reason why the professional practitioner should not see eye to eye with his clerical client. The only person who may have reason to becloud the issue is the merchant.

The battle would be easily won if, first of all, we would forego the expensive luxury of purchasing those dubious and valueless products that have flooded our churches only because of the continued indifference and because of the superb salesmanship that is the stock-in-trade of the ecclesiastical merchant. When you have reached the bottom there is no place to go but up. Then we could begin to pay some attention to artists.

I doubt that many will question the need for reform in the matter of religious art. It is here that we run into the plaint: "Well and good, but we cannot possibly afford the services of those artists you have in mind." I can assure any prospective client that among the host of artists and craftsmen whose talents are now channeled in secular work, there are many who would ask for nothing better than to work for the Church. They are now largely uninterested because they do not feel free or able or willing to lower their standards. Many would be willing to devote their talents to the furtherance of that beauty which we seek in the house of God, but they maintain the conviction that they should be treated as persons worthy of their hire and be respected for their art. I am convinced that, given opportunities, these artists and craftsmen could greatly enhance the beauty of our churches, and do it without increasing the general budget of any reasonably large operation.

This question of religious art is not insoluble once we admit the need for some measure of reform. If we want good work, we can have it; if we really want to commission competent and talented artists we can do so and we can find them in all parts of this land (without going abroad—which, by the way, is merely another way to evade responsibility). If we want to avoid the mistakes of the past we need only by-pass those responsible for them; if we accept the necessity of paying hand-somely for objects of daily use we should not object to paying the artist a fair and decent compensation. All this will even-tually redound to the credit of the parish, and many of us, as parishioners, will see in our churches evidence of that tradi-tional beauty we so like to read about in history books.

In this connection it is interesting to note two churches, in which all details were carefully studied by the pastors, that were planned with strict regard for rubrical law (with the ex-ception of a few details beyond the immediate control of these pastors). One is Saint Mark's Church, Burlington, Vermont; the other, at the opposite corner of the country, is Saint Joseph's, Sunnyside, Washington. In both cases, the pastor began with the liturgy and planned the church accordingly. An obvious solution, some will say; of course, but it is surpris-ing how often churches are planned according to norms hardly liturgical, only because those *un*liturgical norms have been consecrated by compounding mistake upon mistake.

In Burlington, Father William A. Tennien had definite ideas that resulted in an altar in the center of the church, enabling him to celebrate Mass facing the people, an innovation that seems to have been accepted without any fuss by his congre-gation. Theoretically, an altar in the center of the plan is a good idea but only, as in the case of Saint Mark's, when three arms of the plan are given over to the people, the fourth arm being taken up by the sacristy, the choir, pulpit, and side altar. In Sunnyside, Father Reinhold has placed the baptistry on center with the altar, and the main entrance is through a *side* narthex. He has also provided for a small side chapel for daily Mass in his community of scattered parishioners, and for a choir flanking the sanctuary. All appurtenances in both churches—altar, tabernacle, sanctuary light, candlesticks, shrines, etc.—are of modest materials but are well designed and well executed. Within the means available, both pastors have produced churches that reflect the advance of the Church in the revival of liturgical and religious art in this country.

In the crypt of the Archabbey at Latrobe, Pennsylvania, under the direction of Dom Quentin Schaut, paintings and wood-carved reliefs have been placed above a number of the many altars; recently, a set of mosaic Stations of the Cross, by Louisa Jenkins, were placed in the crypt of another Benedictine Abbey, at Mount Angel, Oregon. Such examples of first-rate work can be found in many places and many more could eventually be executed and placed in our churches, abbeys, seminary chapels, convents, and colleges.

The future of religious art in the United States can flower ultimately if we have the *will* to sponsor the work of our own artists. Here and there the seeds are being planted. A little late, perhaps, but surely American Catholics are reclaiming their lost traditions.

Walter Kerr

MOVIES

B AD TASTE is not one of the seven deadly sins, and nobody is going to hell for having preferred "Quo Vadis" over "God Needs Men." But neither is there any wisdom in elevating bad taste to the level of a virtue, or in confusing it with virtue itself. And it does seem to me that American Catholic criticism of the popular arts—especially the sort of criticism that is generally meted out to the motion picture—is rapidly driving itself into just such an unattractive, and philosophically untenable, corner.

However inadvertently, and with whatever genuine concern for the moral health of its membership, the Church in this country has permitted itself to become identified with the well-meaning second-rate. In effect, it has seemed to say: "I don't care what the quality of the art work is, so long as its content is innocuous, or perhaps favorably disposed in our direction."

In the most publicized Catholic "art" award of 1952, the Christophers selected "Quo Vadis." This essay in calculated vulgarity represented, we were told, "creative work of enduring significance." It was "outstanding," not merely because it threw a certain number of Christians to a certain number of lions, but because it lived up to the highest esthetic "standards." The truth, of course, slips out; in presenting the award, Father Keller immediately launched into praise of the film for showing "how a handful of human beings, fired with the love and truth of Christ, were able to overcome the might of Pagan Rome." The esthetic norm is clearly the proselytizing content, if, with a little effort of the imagination, "Quo Vadis" could be considered as really having proselytizing content.

But this avowal—that Christians ought to like "Quo Vadis" because "Quo Vadis" likes Christians—was not a frank one. There was the additional insistence that the film's special pleading, its fairly dim and remote hoeing of the Catholic row, be equated with artistic merit. Because Saint Peter had been given a certain amount of footage in the production, this form of logic demands that therefore the movie in question be praised for its craftsmanship.

The intention is virtuous; the execution must therefore not be called into question, must indeed be lauded as supremely desirable. The makers of motion pictures were explicitly urged to go on in the same vein, with the assurance that they would thereby arrive at unparalleled esthetic glories. The *Christopher News Notes* announced that "outstanding personalities in the entertainment and literary fields . . . predict that if similar Christopher Awards are made for the next three or four years, they may do more to stimulate high quality work in these spheres of influence than any other single factor."

The sort of judgment which at best reveals an alarming innocence of the very texture of art, and which at worst smacks suspiciously of cant, has pretty much become rule-of-thumb for the American Catholic moviegoer. A film featuring a saint is a film of majestic technical excellence. A film showing a nun driving a jeep is a superbly made comedy. A film embracing a jolly priest, a self-sacrificing Catholic mother, and an anti-

Communist message must be defended in the diocesan press from those irresponsible esthetes and conspiratorial leftists—and even worse, those maverick Catholics—who have had the meanness and the malice to question it.

When there is no recent film of obviously Catholic sympathies—no priest in the pulpit, no nun in the backfield, no early-Christian Deborah Kerr in the jaws of a Technicolor lion—the next-best bet, in the current practice of Catholic criticism, is to play it safe. An earlier Christopher Award—I am not really out after the Christophers; they got out there by themselves—went to "The Father of the Bride." Now "The Father of the Bride" was a pleasant little film, certainly a harmless little film. That it represented the peak of creative achievement, of imaginative artistry, in its given year is, however, fairly doubtful. (If one wanted to be parochially picky about it, one might even raise some doubt about its suitability for an explicitly Catholic award; if the film reflected any social concept at all, it reflected precisely that slick, sentimental, materialistic concept of the two-child, two-car family against which pulpit orators have so long and richly fulminated.) But it was a film that was kind to babies, kind to parents, generally optimistic about the domestic scene. It was therefore qualified for praise on the highest level of esthetic achievement. The identification of good will with good work is commonplace in the Catholic press. Unfortunately, the sort of art which Catholics are urged to admire is commonplace, too—and the power which Catholic spokesmen have come to wield over the motion picture even more commonplace than it need have been.

The penalties of this inverted esthetic—the notion that what is pure is also necessarily perfect—have thus been double. Catholic taste in motion pictures has been frozen at the "unobjectionable," or purity-with-popcorn level, a level that if pursued down the ages, would have called into question nearly every literary or dramatic masterpiece ever produced. (We need not think of such rowdy samples as "Volpone" or "Tartuffe," a "Phèdre" or a "Hamlet" will do.) And the American film has, through the rigid circumscriptions of the production code and the terrors of an unfavorable Legion of Decency rating, been dissuaded from attempting anything complex enough in the way of human behavior to serve as the basis for a new masterpiece.

The first of these penalties—the petrifaction of taste—cannot seem of much moment to men whose urgent concern is the saving of souls. Yet it has far more serious consequences than many an honest moralist realizes: it discredits the entire Catholic intellectual tradition. The man who had been to see "Quo Vadis" might reach certain conclusions: that the "Catholic" concept of art is a decidedly primitive one; that it probably rests on similarly primitive philosophical principles; that the Church, when its true colors are showing, is essentially antipathetic to the creative spirit, essentially in league with the vulgar.

The fact that each of these assumptions is thoroughly false, and would seem strange indeed to an Augustine, an Aquinas, or a Newman, is nothing for which the contemporary observer can be held responsible; the impression is thrust upon him, paraded before him, drummed in his ears by the most vocal Catholic spokesmen in the field.

And this conviction that bad taste among Catholics is due to an ineradicable defect deep down in the Catholic philosophical mind leads to new damage: it tends to shut off Catholic intellectual influence altogether. We hear a great deal about the "influence" Catholicism has had on the American screen. We forget that this influence has been wholly of one

kind: the influence of the pressure group. The Legion of Decency is an economic weapon; the production code was written
under the standing fear of boycott. Neither represents an intellectual victory in the sense that an esthetic principle has
been stated with such clarity and force as to bring about free
assent. The only persuasiveness we have been able to whip up
is the persuasiveness of the dollar.

The barbed-wire barriers of the production code may be
up; but the lines of communication are down. The theatergoer,
the critic, or the creative artist who stands outside the Church
looking in, sees only a forbidding tangle of precaution and
proscription, over which hovers a halo of bad taste. He does
not notice much lively discussion of esthetic value; indeed, he
will quickly discover that "esthetic" is a bad word in vast areas
of the Catholic press. He does not notice much effort to liberal-
ize parochial taste; indeed, he will quickly find most such effort
labeled "art for art's sakeism." He will nowhere run across any
frank recognition of home truths—such as that a work of art
may be perfectly clean and perfectly terrible. That he should
feel vaguely uncomfortable in this environment is understandable. That he should reject it is perhaps inevitable. That
he should feel, in rejecting it, that he is thereby rejecting the
whole body of Catholic thought on the arts, the central content of Catholic philosophy itself, is tragic. Yet by stubbornly
praising what is safely banal, by strenuously encouraging a
low level of taste, we are fostering such an impression.

Our fear that any recognition of the claims of the "esthetic"
may undermine the Catholic accomplishment to date, our re-
luctance to encourage any study of the nature of art as art,
our insistence that the Catholic contribution stop dead at the
cautionary level, have also brought about the second penalty

mentioned above: the discouragement of the creative film-maker pursuing the ultimate possibilities of his craft.

Again this is going to seem no serious matter to the man whose whole concern is prudence. The motion picture, this man may tell himself, is probably never going to amount to much, anyway; the dangers of Hollywood indiscretion are greater than the possible damage that may be done to an exceptional film here and there; was Hollywood ever very "esthetic" in the first place?

To anyone who remembers the standard M-G-M scenario shortly before the Legion of Decency came into existence—Joan Crawford is Clark Gable's mistress for six reels and triumphantly marries him in the seventh—this attitude may yet evoke a twinge of sympathy, a shrug of endorsement. But cynicism is no friend of truth, despair no incentive to achievement. It is never enough to substitute one vulgarity for another. Unless one makes an esthetically informed and basically sympathetic approach to a medium, there is a likelihood of replacing one sort of error with another sort; even the "prudent" make mistakes. In the case of the production code, the failure to balance prudence with knowledge would seem to have resulted in some curious philosophical constructions. The notion, for instance, that sin is always, and very precisely, punished in this life would not appear to be Catholic dogma; yet it is at Catholic insistence that the screen echoes and re-echoes the concept.

A few years ago Warners remade the old Maugham story "The Letter." In the original, as I remember it, the heroine's infidelity (and her subsequent murder of her lover) was ironically paid off by the prospect of an eternal hell in the company of a husband who now knew the truth. In the remake, under the code, it was necessary to dispatch the adulteress by

having a handy native girl slip a knife into her. The new end-
ing was also, it seems to me, morally simple-minded, reflect-
ing a remarkable, primitive understanding of the ways of God
and men. (It might be mentioned that it was now also necessary to kill off the native girl, instituting a chain of blood
vengeance unknown since the *Oresteia.*) There are more subtle, and more terrifying, punishments than the code quite en-
visions. There are also more "Catholic" ones.

To take another example more or less at random, the filming
of "A Streetcar Named Desire" found Stella Kowalski leaving
her loutish husband. There was sound enough reason for leaving this man, even apart from his table manners: he had dis-
honored his wife's sister. But the code that demanded this
climax was written under Catholic influence, with the guidance
of Catholic spokesmen. Is it actually the Catholic position that
a wife must leave her husband for infidelity? And what, in this
eye-for-an-eye, tooth-for-a-tooth world, has become of the virtue of charity?

Much more importantly, what has become of that profound
little maxim Paul Claudel has quoted: "God writes straight
with crooked lines"? This is pretty much the crux of the matter, so far as the making of films, or the creation of any sort
of art, is concerned. The great artist, be he Claudel or Tolstoy,
Racine or Shakespeare, follows the bent of human nature honestly through its aberrant as well as its generous impulses,
through its virtues and vices alike, until all fall into place in
a complex, but truthful, pattern. The lines are crooked, the
ultimate vision straight. What is both wrong and foolish about
the present production code is that it insists that God write
straight with straight lines, that He attend strictly to business
as the business is conceived by an either/or, black-and-white,
pay-as-you-go mentality.

Art without crooked lines is unnatural art—inevitably inferior art. And in its production not only the creative mind is betrayed; the Catholic mind, in its fullness, in its scope, in its centricity, is betrayed as well. Because we are terrified that any admission of the legitimate claims of art will send us all dancing off into the perilous realms of "art for art's sake"—though there are a dozen intermediate esthetic positions—we are moving closer and closer to the sort of stand that might well be described as "vulgarity for God's sake." I am not sure that God is well served by any dishonesty, by any distortion of the world He made—not even that distortion which enables us to "take the children."

None of this is meant to say that the motion picture, or any other art form, should be exempted from legitimate criticism. Nor is it meant to say that the motion picture should be exempted from such criticism as may be considered specifically Catholic, specifically drawn from that body of wisdom which the Church has nurtured through the ages. I am not suggesting that a Catholic has no right to raise his voice or even to make use of such pressure tactics as a democratic society actually grants him. I do not really mean to hold out the hope that the Hollywood we know is a seething ferment of crushed genius that will, the moment the code is liberalized or the Legion relaxes, burst forth with a hundred magnificent films.

It is rather to say—as Catholics are so often and so honestly heard to say—that every right involves a responsibility. We have loudly asserted our rights where the screen is concerned; I am not sure that we have accepted, or even realized, our responsibilities, that we have behaved with full justice toward that gift of God that is known as "art," toward the artist himself, toward the central tradition of Catholic thought, or even, sometimes, toward the working intellect itself. We have, for instance, talked ourselves into a corner, and into a code, which would automatically prohibit filming certain works of Mauriac, Claudel, Bernanos, or Greene. Perversely, we have as Catholics made it difficult for the most distinguished—and the most influential—Catholic creative voices of our time to gain access to this particular medium.

Erik von Kuehnelt-Leddihn

A EUROPEAN VIEW OF
CATHOLIC EXTREMISTS

B Y THIS time "reaction" has become such a glib label that
one has to define it before applying it. A reactionary—if
the rules of etymology mean anything—is a person opposing
by principle or habit, knowingly and methodically, all currently dominant notions and ideas, or, at least, the very spirit
of the times, the *Zeitgeist* as it is reflected in the mind of the
reactionary himself.

The term "reactionary," like the term "conservative," has a
meaning only in reference to *other* trends, ideas, or situations.
Yet whereas the conservative is a man saying "yes" to a given
period and its standard set of values, which, rightly or wrongly,
he wants to conserve, the reactionary's stand is primarily negative. Not only does he reject the present, but also the future,
whose dim outlines he seems to visualize with growing distaste. Thus the Catholic Reactionary, endowed with a pitiless
eye, sees only the evil aspects of our world, which he opposes
either with real fury or in a spirit of sour petulance and disdain.

We have no reason to doubt that the Catholic Reactionary,
no less than his opposite number, the Catholic Assimilationist,
is motivated by a genuine worry about the future of the
Church. Without any genuine hope for a final victory of truth

over untruth, of justice over crime, of Saint Michael over Satan, he thinks that the cause of the Mystical Body is best served by a strategy based on spiritless retreats and intermittent vengeful counterattacks.

Whoever truly knows Catholicism in its theological, philosophical, and historic aspects will wonder where the roots of this odd phenomenon, the Catholic Reactionary, actually are to be found. After all, change (in the sense of development and addition), movement, and variation have always been the main characteristics of Catholicism, which Karl Barth considers to be "basically dialectic." Saint Vincent of Lerins emphasized "Catholic progressivism" as early as the fifth century when he wrote in his *Commonitorium* about the *profectus Ecclesiae.* A growing volume of the faith militates against a static concept. There exists, moreover, a growth of the Church in a geographic sense, a constant succession of generations, a ceaseless shedding and assuming of a vast diversity of cultural forms. Catholicism in general and ecclesiastic forces in particular have been the most dynamic factors in our cultural and intellectual evolution ever since the Church was able to leave the dark recesses of the catacombs. A cursory glance at the Old World will reveal that there is hardly anything that did not spring from Catholicism directly or indirectly: neither Luther nor Calvin, neither Rousseau nor Robespierre, neither Marx nor Proudhon can be imagined without a Christian-Catholic "prehistory."

Yet at the end of the eighteenth century and in the nineteenth century the faith became truly a *religio depopulata;* it was swept from the market place and banished from the big cities with their pulsating life; it found refuge largely in the tiny circles of a tradition-bound nobility and in the unchanged quietness of the rural districts. The newly emerging proletariat and the middle classes broke with the faith as they had broken with the past; whatever remained of it among the burghers was soon marred by a highly negative spirit made up of a certain pharisaical self-righteousness mixed with a combative drive to destroy, through mechanical means, the evil of a world in apostasy.

In this attitude we see an element which preceded the establishment of the Catholic ghetto of the last one hundred and fifty years, a permanent lure which the Church had to fight almost from the moment of its inception. Symbolized by the Sword of Peter which severed the ear of Malchus, this is the terrible temptation, often barely resisted: to establish God's Kingdom through sheer power—with or without the aid of the secular arm.

Naturally the origins of the Catholic Reactionary cannot be explained simply in the light of purely historical or sociological circumstances. To identify him exclusively with the actively Catholic minority in the urban middle class would be most unjust. The bourgeois spirit itself is by no means tied to a social layer or estate; it can affect royalty and proletarians, artists and priests.

Yet the Catholic Reactionary is a "type," so formed almost from birth. He is a person to whom the Church and the faith are not a final fulfillment but an armor without which he simply could not exist. It was his fortune to have been born into the Catholic Church or to have found her accidentally on his way, after another armor, for some reason, had to be dispensed with. Thus it is not the essence of the Church that attracts him, not the Grace inherent in the sacraments tying him to the Mystical Body, not the appeal "Ye are Priests and Kings" made by Saint Thomas (and also by Peter) to all believers, not the freedom, the greatness, nay, even the elegance

and the humor imparted to us by truth everlasting. These
hardly affect the Catholic Reactionary, who is primarily moved
by the organizational aspects of the Church Militant, with its
laws, rules, and bylaws, which he tends to place above the
Ten Commandments, the Sermon on the Mount, and the message of the Epistles.

The Catholic Reactionary is a man of prohibitions and
"don'ts," a man who has reversed Saint Thomas's scale of virtues, placing charity lowest, ranking the moral behind the intellectual virtues, and locating chastity at the top of the ladder,
high above fortitude or justice. Affection, generosity, intellec-
tuality play for him merely a minor role. "Prudence" (with a
liberal admixture of cowardice and fear) is his watchword.
A battle nobly lost he cherishes less than a cheap victory.
And there is nothing he is more afraid of than "scandal," taking this word in its everyday, not its theological, sense, since
it is "appearing" and not "being" he is most concerned with.
He has never accepted the words of Saint Bernard: *Melius est
ut scandalum oriatur, quam ut veritas relinquatur.*

Whereas the Catholic Assimilationist and Leftist causes
great trouble by sowing confusion in the ranks of the faithful,
the Catholic Reactionary with his aggressiveness and emphasis
on the accidentals of the faith is one of the main reasons why
so many of the very best *extra muros* are being kept outside
the Perennial City. The Catholic Reactionary is unable to
adopt whatever is positive, whatever is true and lasting outside of the Church, because he ignores (and wants to ignore)
the fact that the Jansenist thesis of the impossibility of Grace
outside of the Mystical Body has been condemned by the
popes.

It is not surprising that the Catholic Reactionary gets fright-
ened by any "trading with the enemy," which to him smacks

of treason. No "association with infidels" for him! And so small is his self-confidence that he avoids all contacts with the very persons most desperately in need of the light of truth.

It is no wonder that this is so, since the Catholic Reactionary believes in an explanation of history that can only be called the "conspiratorial thesis." He sees the whole world around his beleaguered ghetto as an intricate network of conspiracies. "Liberals," Masons, Protestants, Orthodox Jews, Communists, Socialists, crypto-fascists, manufacturers of contraceptives, feminists, designers of bathing suits, movie moguls, yellow journalists, Satan worshipers, Zionists, modern artists, agents of foreign powers, biologists—all, in his view, are joined in an unholy alliance whose purpose is to destroy the Church. The fact that on various occasions *some* of these groups actually do line up together against Rome in the eyes of the Catholic Reactionary is valid proof of a permanent secret understanding among them.

Here we encounter another trait of the Catholic Reactionary—nationalism. Marxists *profess* to be internationalists. Since the Catholic Reactionary always takes his cue from the enemy's pretensions, he therefore adopts nationalism and "patriotism," forgetting that his Church stands above the nations. The only redeeming feature here lies in the fact that it precludes the possibility of a Fifth International—the dark specter of a globe-girdling alliance of all Catholic Reactionaries.

Nationalism attracts the Catholic Reactionary through its narrowness and parochialism, the chances it offers to be "agin" others. He is a patrioteer. If other nations also happen to be Catholic, their Catholicism, of course, is highly suspect. He is a man of monopolies. His nation, and his nation alone, has a lien on the Church, and it hardly needs stressing that the institutions of his country all enjoy a very special blessing from God Almighty. If his nation is a monarchy (or has recently been one), kingship is divinely ordained. If it happens to be a republic of long standing, democracy is Our Lord's command. But true happiness beckons to him only if he can drag religion into party politics, because then his partisanship can reach a higher pitch and can be raised to the level of hysterics.

Apart from the foes within and without the Church he is certain that the archenemy of mankind is sex. He is a knight errant for "decency," fighting "sin" as one fights a dragon; for him these terms have an exclusively sexual meaning. He also succeeds splendidly in using his indignation about the sexual trespasses of others to manifest toward the wayward a pent-up wrath that sometimes appears to be caused by a secret, subconscious envy.

The absence of sympathy on the part of the Catholic Reactionary is often combined with a tremendous vanity about his own "temperance" and "modesty." When it comes to reading matter, he is all for a strict censorship, but his provincialism makes him singularly unfit to distinguish between art and pornography.

He would receive a great jolt if he were to study Church art of past ages or to travel widely, thus getting an opportunity to see Eros or even Sex represented *ad maiorem Dei gloriam*—often, but not always, survivals of his own dear "good old times." He then would behold the obscene demons over the gates of Bourges' Saint Etienne, Saint Mary Magdalen's beautiful torso in the Cathedral of Pisa, the frescoes of Vasari in the *Duomo* of Florence, the bare, marble bodies of the kings and queens of France in Saint Denis, the frescoes of Michelangelo in the Sistine Chapel, the naked Saint Catherine of Alexandria broken over the wheel in a modern stained-glass window of Fribourg's Saint Nicholas, not to mention the details of Saint Agatha's festival in Catania.

If a man, the Catholic Reactionary is usually a misogynist. His female counterpart is frequently an ardent feminist. Their nationalism enters into a curious alliance with their puritan Jansenism: they believe all foreigners to be sex fiends while their own nation figures in their mind as a wellspring of chastity.

The Catholic Reactionary is, naturally, opposed to organized labor, but he is also against the aristocracy, the intellectuals, the army officers, artists, and seamen. He dislikes diplomats, journalists, circus performers, night-club singers, and skiing champions. He suspects comedians and cartoonists. In his eyes they are not "respectable." At one and the same time he is a middle-of-the-roader and a believer in absolutes or, at least, in one absolute: mediocrity and its pitiless defense.

The Catholic Reactionary loves policemen and gendarmes. He strongly favors conscription and almost every form of regimentation and regulation. But his most ardent enthusiasm is reserved for "the clergy." He does not see in the individual priest a man who has shouldered a very special cross. He does not recognize in him a man who has risked almost everything in a divine game in which a glowing sanctity and a particular dry rot of the soul are the frightening alternatives spared to most laymen. No, the priest to him is a master who takes every decision out of his hands, issues infallible pronouncements on all conceivable subjects, and has absolute command in the defense of the beleaguered ghetto.

More than any priest or bishop, more than a hundred Cardinal Seguras, the Catholic Reactionary is guilty of making anticlericalism—the permanent alibi of anti-Catholicism—ap-

pear to be a plausible attitude. The Catholic Reactionary is
not really keen on conquest, but on preservation and defense.
Hence his enthusiasm for censorship, boycotts, and the demonstration of numerical strength. He is not the son of a free
Church, but rather the sycophant, the informer, the flunky of
a small, cornered sect.

If he merely wanted to put the clock back, one still would
respect him in a way. Don Quixote, after all, is a tragic and
lovable figure. But the Catholic Reactionary is an enthusi-
astic distributor of blinkers, muzzles, handcuffs, black glasses,
apron strings, gags, and earmuffs. His eyes shine when he
hears that somewhere in the world the arm of the law has
intervened in order to insure the victory of faith and morals.
If Protestant missionaries are ejected from a town on Lake
Titicaca, or attendance at Mass on weekdays is made compulsory in a school, if an immoral book is banned in Boston,
if a meeting of "freethinkers" is disrupted with stink bombs
or with beer mugs, or if a leftist paper is suspended, he seems
almost mystically transported. His joy reaches new heights
when he hears that the police have issued a bylaw regarding
the length of bathing suits or that a stricter censorship code
has been promulgated in Hollywood, because he believes that
ethics can be enforced by regulations and morality measured
with rules.

The Catholic Reactionary has limitless veneration for the
Middle Ages in which he sees the fulfillment of Catholicism.
From humanism he instinctively recoils, and to him the Renaissance is nothing but paganism incarnate "preparing the
Reformation" (which actually was a late medieval revolt
against the Renaissance, *against* Humanism, *against* this Catholic synthesis of truth and beauty, of the intellect and the
senses). Yet if by some magic he were to find himself sud-

226

denly in the Middle Ages, he would be made dreadfully unhappy by so tough, "immoral," intellectual, and anticlerical a period; he surely would go down on his knees praying to be whisked "back where he came from"—to the mid-twentieth century? Oh no, to 1888.

In his tastes the Catholic Reactionary is "conservative," that is, he sticks to the notions of 1888. Modern art to him is (for want of a better label) "bolshevistic" and a modern church nothing less than blasphemy. The only modernization he will tolerate is a coat of phosphorescent material over crucifixes—of a design that repelled Lourdes visitors way back under Napoleon III. North of the Alps, the only type of church in which he gladly worships must be "medieval," Romanesque, or Gothic in style—preferably in the 1888 edition with a Beuronian interior decoration, a linoleum floor, and an altar adorned with woodwork reminding one of sugar-coated pretzels.

In the forms of his worship, the Catholic Reactionary has an unerring nose for the nonessentials of his faith. An addict of blessed medals, he finds the zenith of his faith in endless novenas, in the reading of doubtful tracts and even more suspect hagiographies, in the blind belief in fake "miracles" and unauthentic "prophecies," following his natural bent toward a spurious mysticism. Thus he oscillates among an avoidance of the genuinely supernatural, an attraction to the darkest forms of superstition, an infatuation with pure magic, and a real obsession with mediocrity masquerading as "moderation."

He has a few glib catch-phrases always on hand with which he hopes to deal with all situations, as, for instance, "I'm all for liberty, but not for license!" Not only does he cover cowardice with a false humility when occasion arises, by uttering a clarion call to "prudence," but when he feels a real resistance mounting, he carefully avoids offering a frank opinion. In such a case he will merely cite "authorities."

The theology of the Catholic Reactionary shows up very well in his conversations. It is a theology that places sin in the center and wildly rotates around this point. Saint Augustine's *"Dilige et fac quod vis,"* the great trust enwrapped by the burning love for God, has given way to the scrupulous Bishop Jansenius' sad epigones. Obviously one is bound in duty to drive for personal salvation, but the best road to heaven is the Holy Folly of the Cross, the surrender to absolute charity—not a constant morbid introspection (the scrupulous person teases God, said Father Faber) nor an ingenious bookkeeping of sins, indulgences, good works, and merits.

Actually this kind of "theology" in its acute unconsciousness is satanocentric; it sees the world peopled by a race largely marked out for damnation, a world full of demons and forerunners of Anti-Christ. The Catholic Reactionary visualizes himself in solitary purity and righteousness, and shares the feelings of Tertullian (an early, very gifted Catholic Reactionary), who said that the source of the greater happiness for the departed in heaven will be the sight of the Roman emperors roasting in hell.

The Catholic Reactionary is marked by a freezing absence of humor. Saint Thomas considered the lack of mirth to be positively sinful, and if you cited this fact to the Catholic Reactionary, he undoubtedly would break out into a dutiful but vacant grin from time to time. There would be no resonance in his heart, for his eye is blind to the comic incongruities of a fallen world.

He is a mournful middle-of-the-roader, this Catholic Reactionary. Without knowing it, he is one of the most bitter enemies of the Church, a real obstacle to its expansion and, as a negative factor in its whole existence, comparable to his antagonist on the opposite end of the scale, the Assimilationist.

The basic, positive motives of the Catholic Reactionary and of the Catholic Assimilationist, curiously enough, are identical. They both want to "save" the Church. The Reactionary is overimpressed with the power of Satan and his cohorts. He has not grasped the nature of the Catholic's abiding mission to take possession of this world entrusted to us by God, to depose the false Prince of this world and inaugurate the rule of Christ the King. The Catholic Assimilationist, on the other hand, believes the only salvation is for the Church to throw herself to the mercy of all the dazzling and dynamic movements of the times. Whereas the ideal of the Catholic Reactionary is a Church eternally at anchor (if not in dry dock), the Catholic Assimilationist is in favor of letting her drift on the high seas of history. He believes implicitly in the goodness of all winds, waves, and currents.

The dark suspicion of a perennial diabolical conspiracy against all real values is characteristic of the Catholic Reactionary; a naïve belief in the intrinsic worth and excellence of almost the whole contemporary scene is the central dogma of the Assimilationist. The sneering arrogance, the narrow "monopolism" of the Reactionary are balanced by the melancholic inferiority complex of the Assimilationist. The latter, moreover, is tortured by a profound perplexity; he has to accept the fact that all basic truths are part and parcel of the Deposit of the Faith, yet everything noble, everything worthwhile, everything pointing to the future seems to grow outside the walls of the Catholic fold. With our correct premises we Catholics have done very little, he believes; we are forever backing the wrong horse. In the two thousand years of our history about all we have done, in his view, was to persecute the Jews in the Middle Ages, produce lecherous popes in the Renaissance, pander to degenerate monarchs during the *ancien régime*, favor fascism, illiteracy, child labor, capitalism, disease, and backwardness, withhold civic rights from women, mix religion with politics, and carry corruption to the four corners of the world. The seed of revelation and dogma, so the Assimilationist sadly decides, has ripened only *in partibus infidelium*. He looks with envious eyes toward Protestant societies, leftist movements, and to doctrines and ideas found at a considerable distance from our faith. The Bill of Rights, the Declaration of Independence, *Das Kapital*, *J'accuse*, *Totem and Tabu* were not written by Catholic authors. All liberating, progressive, constructive, humane movements and ideas in the last three hundred years grew outside the fold!

Yet to say a word in defense of the Catholic Assimilationist, it should be admitted that all Catholic failures—and undeniably there were and still are many—belong to the category of the *skandalon* (in the theological sense), while the non-Catholic shortcomings do not. Looking at the political aspects of the problem, we have to recognize that the leftist movements before and after the French Revolution and the religious and political aberrations of the last two thousand years actually have to be evaluated as Christian heresies; they are inconceivable without their Catholic roots. (An exception is National Socialism, whose racist aspect is a synthesis of Old Testament notions with the pseudo-science of the biological laboratory.) Whether we are concerned with Jacobinism or sectarian liberalism, with the more moderate Marxism of the West or the aggressive Marxism of the East, without a Christian origin, a Christian "soil," these ideologies could never have blossomed forth. The Inquisitors knew but too well that only the corruption of the best can result in the worst; therefore they acted against those adopting heretical views with a severity absent in their dealings with those who were not Christian at all—with Jews and pagans. Still, the Catholic Assimilationist, trying with the fervor of despair to put his faith under the same denominator as the dynamic collectivistic forces of the day, is actually being faced with a rather tempting proposition: he is building a bridge from ideas and notions fundamentally and solidly Christian to views and trends which, one reluctantly has to admit, have Christian roots and Christian antecedents.

To the Catholic Reactionary these efforts seem monstrous, because in the leftist movements he sees merely the anti-ecclesiastic fixations and, what matters to him less, the anti-Christian admixtures. No wonder he is convinced of the Assimilationist's bad faith; after all, a man or a woman emphasizing individual human rights when the whole community is in danger, a person habitually looking for inspiration among the infidels or exulting over the grain of truth he finds in the theories and teachings of heretics, "radicals," "liberals," "Reds," "modernists," "progressives," etc. can only be a traitor or an opportunist. To the Reactionary such self-denying efforts remain anathema, and this for the reason that as a partisan of his Church he rejects heresies and philosophic aberrations as conflicting with "regulations"—and not essentially as errors. To err is human. Man is neither angel nor beast, but the Catholic Reactionary tries very hard to be a beastly angel. The Assimilationist, on the other hand, dreams of baptizing all leftist movements and ideas from the notions of Tom Paine to the doctrine of Lenin. But heresies, like the heretics themselves, do not stand in need of baptism. What they need is "*con*version" or "*re*version." Only persons or things pagan can be "baptized"—at least in so far as they are "natural" and not diabolic.

The Catholic Reactionary has to be viewed as the presumptuous and priggish-prudish child of the Church, hiding a personal inferiority complex under the mask of aggressiveness. The Assimilationist, on the contrary, is the sad son of the Church who has shouldered the heavy burden of the Cross, which to him is anything but a sweet yoke. If he meets non-Catholics, the uncharitable, confused apologetics of the Reactionary become in his mouth shyly muttered apologies. And while the Reactionary is fully convinced he is the backbone and glory of the Church, the Assimilationist finds himself in the sorrowful role of a stepchild. This state of affairs can well be explained by the fact that rarely are there theological principles motivating Catholic Reaction, a cancerous growth connected with the *ecclesiastic* structure. But roots of Catholic Assimilationism reach into much deeper layers, since Assimilationism is a strategic mistake on a *theological* basis.

Thus it is difficult to attack the Reactionary with arguments drawn from papal documents. Seemingly an injustice is here being perpetrated; from Rome the Assimilationist frequently receives severe injunctions or admonitions, whereas, we have to confess, there are no solemn pronouncements of the Supreme Pontiff against prudishness or a "Catholic" lack of charity. (Hence the unique character of the Boston Feeney case, which received attention on the highest level since, in spite of its Reactionary and rigorist aspect, it dealt with theological rather than with ecclesiastic issues.)

While the Catholic Reactionary, sinning against fundamental Christian precepts, will get his just reward largely on the other side of the grave, the Assimilationist, often a tragic rather than comic figure, spends much of his life under a cloud of suspicion. And if, unlike Lamennais, Buonaiuti, or Loisy, who finally went off the deep end, he remains loyal to the Church, the unkind treatment meted out to him will also decrease his pride in his faith and accentuate his sense of personal tragedy. Should he really be shaken in his religious convictions the Reactionaries around him will be filled with glee and ill-concealed satisfaction. "I told you so," they will explain joyfully, and emphasize the need for "greater watchfulness" and the necessity to "tighten the ranks"—which, in reality, means the tightening of a strait jacket around the Mystical Body. Nor should it be forgotten that while the Reactionary is treated by the world with a mixture of loathing and amusement, the Assimilationist is approached with a complete absence of respect if not with contempt. His bridge-building efforts are thoroughly misunderstood and he appears as a man who lacks the courage to sever the last ties with a "backward Church."

Here, however, is the place again to remind the reader of the old temptation facing the Church—the temptation to use sheer force in order to establish God's Kingdom on earth. I have already mentioned Peter and the ear of Malchus. And it is Peter, Christ's first Vicar on earth, who all through the ages is the constant despair of the Assimilationist. No wonder, because, like the Reactionary, the Assimilationist is a perfectionist who never becomes reconciled to the fact that the Catholic Church is the Petrine Church.

For better or worse, there is no such thing as a Johannean or Pauline Church. Christ, for reasons of His own, chose Peter as His representative and gave him the Power of the Keys. Peter, our first Holy Father, to whom Our Lord once had addressed the memorable words "Get thee behind me, Satan," was not, as far as we can see, the most saintly of the apostles. He was a liar, a hypocrite, and almost an assassin. The painful memories of the Malchus incident, the crowing cock, and the too highly "diplomatic" behavior in Antioch accompany the history of Holy Mother Church through the ages. Peter is *pêcheur et pécheur, piscator et peccator,* fisherman and sinner. Catholics are not a set of perfectionists. We form the Church of saints *and* sinners.

Yet whereas the Reactionary tries to deny all the blemishes on the human face of the Church, the Assimilationist uses them to bolster up the Great Catholic Inferiority Complex and thus ends by denying that we have any right whatsoever to pass judgment on other ideologies or movements. We all know the version of history so popular among the Reactionaries according to which every downfall of the Church, every setback and calamity, has been due merely to the evil conspiracies of dark conventicles, secret societies, and satanic individuals—a version bolstered up by a whole class of "historians" in English-speaking countries who are a trifle too eager to offset the ill effects of the Froude-Kingsley-Prescott-Lea-Macaulay school of historiography. Yet our Assimilationist prefers to be fooled by these classic anti-Catholic propagandists rather than by the good Catholic *terribles simplificateurs* whose books were stuffed down his throat during college years. How presumptuous, he would exclaim, brazenly to condemn these misguided idealists of the Old World who with the help of the guillotine, the gas chamber, and the bullet in the nape of the neck occasionally have engaged in social engineering. They may have erred, but so have we. At least they have tried to ride the waves of the future. All we have done was to help put the clock back.

A naïve partisanship, as we can see, is by no means the monopoly of the Reactionary. Hell-bent upon establishing the

Kingdom of God with mechanical means, either by well-organized pressure groups or the successful invocation of the secular arm, he is a miserable psychologist. The doctrinaire liberals are wrong in believing that the spirit will always prevail against brute force. Yet the terror and brutality necessary to establish and uphold a lasting order against an intelligent and serious opposition is something not even our Catholic Reactionary could tolerate. The Assimilationist, on the other hand, trying to tie the Church to secular ideologies is a bad philosopher and theologian.

At heart both the Reactionary and the Assimilationist are illiberal; both are enemies of freedom—the Assimilationist with his implicit urge to tie down his faith and his Church to secular movements and interests, if not to fashions and fads; the Reactionary with his double complex of active and passive persecution. In their own ways these two crybabies are both subject to the world and the spirit of time, because they have apostatized from the essence of Christianity, which is sovereignty and freedom, *i.e.*, the stand above time and space that alone promises the mastery of history. The Assimilationist has failed because he got stuck in a given historical period and is now being carried away by the currents of "contemporary thought," while the Reactionary fervently wants to represent the cliff on which the vessels of iniquity will be wrecked. He then rashly assumes that the cliff, on which many a fine little boat has foundered, is identical with the Rock of Saint Peter.

It is difficult to say which one of these two fellows has caused more damage. The Assimilationist, doubtless, sows confusion among some of the faithful, whereas the Reactionary is the live obstacle that prevents so many good people from joining the Church. Not only his views, but frequently also his "irreproachable conduct," exude an aura of holy terror. We can be quite sure that the wicked Renaissance popes did less damage to the Church than the "purifying flame" of the stake.

The Reactionary, owing to his permanent residence within the walls of the ghetto, rarely changes the objectives of his wrathful attacks, while the Assimilationist with his entangling alliances shifts from one enthusiasm to another. Here the law of the vicious circle has always made itself felt in all its iniquity. If, as in France (and even in England), at one end of the Catholic camp, the Reactionaries actively engaged in the immoral silliness of *Antidreyfusisme,* the Assimilationists at the other had decided to make common cause with the intellectual leftovers of the French Revolution, and, a generation later, to feast with the supporters of that international body which behind the façade of a "Worker's Party" has actually established the most terrible tyranny in all history.

All this does not invalidate the fact that the Catholic Assimilationist in his attitude is representing a half-truth. He is right in assuming that bridges can be built where such a thing is feasible, *i.e.,* to islands that geographically can be considered to belong to the Continent of the Faith. The Pope also is a *Pontifex Maximus,* a Supreme Bridge-builder, if we translate this term in a literal sense.

But the Assimilationist ought to be told that though it is legitimate and often a real duty to talk to the "others" even if they are declared enemies, one arranges such meetings on the bridge. Only in the rarest of all cases does one enter their camp. Even if they are temporarily most successful, one has to remember the lines of A. L. Thomas:

A European View of Catholic Extremists

*Le temps sera pour vous
—l'éternité pour nous.*

The balanced Catholic or, to use a term frequently heard on the Continent, the "Christian-who-is-of-age," certainly conforms with Saint Thomas Aquinas's concept of the true Christian. Saint Thomas, in accordance with Apostle Peter's notion (I Peter 2, ix), called all members of the Mystical Body "Priests and Kings." The Catholic, obviously, is a member of a hierarchically organized, authoritarian *Church,* yet as to Catholic *theology* there can be no doubt that it is intrinsically libertarian, resting on the double columns of Free Will and the Primacy of Conscience. In a certain way the Catholic evidently is bound in duty and obedience, but as a member of the Mystical Body he is basically free and self-responsible, a struggling, thinking, distinguishing, and judging Image of God. Nothing has done greater harm to us than the picture (assiduously propagated by some in our midst) of the Catholic as a docile, meek, obedient, poetically simple-minded, easily manageable paragon of all domestic and civic virtues, ideally qualified to serve humbly his ecclesiastic or political taskmasters. Yet to the traveler in time and space such a concept is sheer moonshine. The history of Catholic nations (as that of the Eastern Schismatics and of the Protestants as long as they remained "orthodox") is one of enormous tensions, revolutions, violent disputes, colossal ideological antagonisms, gripping personal tragedies.

There is a childish notion that Catholics are smoothly functioning automatic vending machines into which you insert neatly packed dogmatic statements that come out at the other end duly stamped and signed. Yet even to revealed truth the Catholic has to give a free and unfettered assent; he has to wrestle with each new tenet of faith. There is, after all, a fundamental difference between the Church in her teaching function and the "Information, Please" type of program. Nor is it the task of the Church to spread happiness here on earth and to make of the Catholics a "mass of happy people." All the Church can do in the last analysis is to give significance and meaning to suffering and prevent despair.

Thus it is evident that the Catholic can never wholly belong to a "camp," especially not to a political camp. All during his life he has to reason and decide with courage and frankness according to his own lights. It may happen that he finds himself unexpectedly allied to a "camp" he does not particularly care for, or lands in the company of strange bedfellows. If an innocent man, for example, is menaced by severe punishment, he will sound his protest even if ten Communist, fascist, Masonic, heretical, or criminal organizations (whatever their silly or sinister motives) are doing likewise. He would, taking another example at random, call for the restoration of a monarchy or advocate a radical agrarian reform regardless of whether this stand would mark him off as a reactionary obscurantist or a "Red." His conviction that such changes are ethically justifiable and would serve the common good is all that really matters. The possibilities of conflicts within his environment are indeed numerous, because there always remain these two elements that will separate him from the crowds: his royal sovereignty in thinking, and the absoluteness of his conscience, which might get him into trouble with everybody—perhaps even with the highest ecclesiastical authorities, witness Saint Joan of Arc or the misguided but saintly Savonarola.

I do not in the least want to insinuate that the ideal Catholic, the Christian-who-is-of-age, will always reach the correct decision or that he is infallible in his judgments. Such infallibility even the Church possesses only in a very narrow field. But the ideal is an "aristocrat" in the deepest sense of the word, as well as a "liberal" in its etymological meaning—and that has nothing to do with either the liberal parties of the nineteenth century or, least of all, with the Manchester school of economics. (Nor should one lose sight of the fact that there is a "Catholic liberalism," but no "liberal Catholicism." In spite of the many aspects and facets of the Catholic faith it does not exist in a variety of "editions.") All this does not imply that we are talking in favor of a Catholic version of Nietzsche's superman, since the real Catholic, called to kingship and priesthood, sees by the same token in his fellow Christians potential or actual kings and priests in whose society he rules humbly and lovingly or serves honestly and proudly. (The work of a "king" is *service*, and even the Pope is *servus servorum Dei*, Servant of God's Servants.)

All this hardly makes the genuine Catholic ideally fitted for membership in a party. The great Catholic figures have proved this sufficiently. One has only to remember Saint Thomas Aquinas, John of the Cross, Teresa of Avila, Blessed Ramon Lull, Reuchlin, Saint Ignatius Loyola, Lacordaire, Montalembert, Rosmini, Newman, Strosmajer, Hecker—some of them had even lingered in ecclesiastical jails, had their ideas condemned, had been hauled before ecclesiastic courts, had been guilty of occasional error; others had been involved in serious troubles with their superiors, had been suspected and vilified, had lived for years under a cloud. Yet little it mattered because they were united with God. Too much has been made of the real Catholic as a being submerged in community. He can be a very lonely person, but he comes near to being a mystic because he stays near to God.

It only remains to acknowledge the fact that the Assimilationist and the Reactionary—neither aristocrats, nor liberals, nor mystics—are in their extreme manifestations true products of the "Church on the Defensive," a label that, in spite of many signs to the contrary, accurately describes the status of the Church in our age.

Notes on Contributors

GEORGE N. SHUSTER, author and educator, is President of Hunter College.

WILLIAM P. CLANCY is an assistant editor of *The Commonweal*.

REINHOLD NIEBUHR, of Union Theological Seminary, is one of America's foremost Protestant theologians.

WILL HERBERG, author of *Judaism and Modern Man*, is a recognized authority on Jewish religious and cultural affairs.

JOHN J. KANE is head of the Department of Sociology at the University of Notre Dame.

JOSEPH M. DUFFY, JR., recently completed his doctoral studies at the University of Chicago and is at present studying in England as a Fulbright Scholar.

JOHN COGLEY is Executive Editor of *The Commonweal*.

DANIEL F. CLEARY was Chairman of the War Claims Commission in Washington, D. C. He died in Chicago, December 5, 1953.

JAMES O'GARA is Managing Editor of *The Commonweal*.

ED MARCINIAK is an officer of the Catholic Labor Alliance in Chicago and Editor of *Work*, a Catholic labor publication.

ED WILLOCK is one of the founders of *Integrity*, a Catholic monthly magazine.

JOSEPH E. CUNNEEN teaches at the College of New Rochelle and is Managing Editor of *Cross Currents*, a quarterly review.

JULIAN PLEASANTS is a research scientist on the staff of the Lobund Institute at the University of Notre Dame.

HENRY RAGO, poet and literary critic, is a member of the faculty of the University of Chicago.

DAN HERR is the president of the Thomas More Association and director of the Thomas More Bookstore in Chicago.

MAURICE LAVANOUX is Secretary of the Liturgical Arts Society.

WALTER KERR was associated for many years with the drama department of the Catholic University of America. He now serves as drama critic for the New York *Herald Tribune*.

ERIK VON KUEHNELT-LEDDIHN is an Austrian sociologist and novelist who lived for many years in the United States. He returns frequently to this country for lecture tours.